Indiana Rules of Cour
Rules of Trial Proced

Including Amendments made through September 8, 2019

'ABLE OF CONTENTS

Rule 1. Scope of the rules

Except as otherwise provided, these rules govern the procedure and practice in all courts of the state of Indiana in all suits of a civil nature whether cognizable as cases at law, in equity, or of statutory origin. They shall be construed to secure the just, speedy and inexpensive determination of every action.

Rule 2. One form of action

(A) There shall be one [1] form of action to be known as "civil action."

(B) The right of a civil action is not merged in a public offense or a public remedy, but may, in all cases, be sought independently of and in addition to the punishment given or relief granted for the public offense.

Rule 3. Commencement of an action

A civil action is commenced by filing with the court a complaint or such equivalent pleading or document as may be specified by statute, by payment of the prescribed filing fee or filing an order waiving the filing fee, and, where service of process is required, by furnishing to the clerk as many copies of the complaint and summons as are necessary.

Rule 3.1 Appearance

(A) Initiating party. At the time an action is commenced, the attorney representing the party initiating the proceeding or the party, if not represented by an attorney, shall file with the clerk of the court an appearance form setting forth the following information:

(1) Name, address, telephone number, FAX number, and e-mail address of the initiating party or parties filing the appearance form;

(2) Name, address, attorney number, telephone number, FAX number, and e-mail address of any attorney representing the party, as applicable;

(3) The case type of the proceeding [Administrative Rule 8(B)(3)];

(4) Unless required by Trial Rule 86(G), a statement that the party will or will not accept service by FAX or by e-mail from other parties;

(5) In domestic relations, Uniform Reciprocal Enforcement of Support (URESA), paternity, delinquency, Child in Need of Services (CHINS), guardianship, and any other proceedings in which support may be an issue, the Social Security Identification Number of all family members;

(6) The caption and case number of all related cases;

(7) Such additional matters specified by state or local rule required to maintain the information management system employed by the court;

(8) In a proceeding involving a protection from abuse order, a workplace violence restraining order, or a no-contact order, the initiating party shall provide to the clerk a public mailing address for purposes of legal service. The initiating party may use the Attorney General Address Confidentiality program established by statute; and

(9) In a proceeding involving a mental health commitment, except 72 hour emergency detentions, the initiating party shall provide the full name of the person with respect to whom commitment is sought and the person's state of residence. In addition, the initiating party shall provide at least one of the following identifiers for the person:

(a) Date of birth;

(b) Social Security Number;

(c) Driver's license number with state of issue and date of expiration;

(d) Department of Correction number;

(e) State ID number with state of issue and date of expiration; or

(f) FBI number.

(10) In a proceeding involving a petition for guardianship, the initiating party shall provide a completed Guardianship Information Sheet in the form set out in Appendix C. The information sheet is a confidential Court Record excluded from public access under Administrative Rule 9.

(B) Responding parties. At the time the responding party or parties first appears in a case, the attorney representing such party or parties, or the party or parties, if not represented by an attorney, shall file an appearance form setting forth the information set out in Section (A) above.

(C) Intervening Parties. At the time the first matter is submitted to the court seeking to intervene in a proceeding, the attorney representing the intervening party or parties, or the intervening party or parties, if not represented by an attorney, shall file an appearance form setting forth the information set out in Section (A) above.

(D) Confidentiality of Court Record Excluded from Public Access. Any appearance form or Court Record defined as not accessible to the public pursuant to Administrative Rule 9(G) shall be filed in the manner required by Administrative Rule 9(G)(5).

(E) Completion and correction of information. In the event matters must be filed before the information required by this rule is available, the appearance form shall be submitted with available information and supplemented when the absent information is acquired. Parties shall promptly advise the clerk of the court of any change in the information previously supplied to the court.

(F) Forms. The Indiana Office of Judicial Administration (IOJA) shall prepare and publish a standard format for compliance with the provisions of this rule.

(G) Service. The Clerk of the Court shall use the information set forth in the appearance form for service by mail, FAX, and e-mail under Trial Rule 5(B).

(H) Withdrawal of Representation. An attorney representing a party may file a motion to withdraw representation of the party upon a showing that the attorney has sent written notice of intent to withdraw to the party at least ten (10) days before filing a motion to withdraw representation, and either:

(1) the terms and conditions of the attorney's agreement with the party regarding the scope of the representation have been satisfied, or

(2) withdrawal is required by Professional Conduct Rule 1.16(a), or is otherwise permitted by Professional Conduct Rule 1.16(b).

An attorney filing a motion to withdraw from representation shall certify the last known address and telephone number of the party, subject to the confidentiality provisions of Sections (A)(8) and (D) above, and shall attach to the motion a copy of the notice of intent to withdraw that was sent to the party.

A motion for withdrawal of representation shall be granted by the court unless the court specifically finds that withdrawal is not reasonable or consistent with the efficient administration of justice.

(I) Temporary or Limited Representation. If an attorney seeks to represent a party in a proceeding before the court on a temporary basis or a basis that is limited in scope, the attorney shall file a notice of temporary or limited representation. The notice shall contain the information set out in Section (A) (1) and (2) above and a description of the temporary or limited status, including the date the temporary status ends or the scope of the limited representation. The court shall not be required to act on the temporary or limited representation. At the completion of the temporary or limited representation, the attorney shall file a notice of completion of representation with the clerk of the court.

Rule 4. Process

(A) Jurisdiction Over Parties or Persons--In General. The court acquires jurisdiction over a party or person who under these rules commences or joins in the action, is served with summons or enters an appearance, or who is subjected to the power of the court under any other law.

(B) Preparation of summons and praecipe. Contemporaneously with the filing of the complaint or equivalent pleading, the person seeking service or his attorney shall furnish to the clerk as many copies of the complaint and summons as are necessary. The clerk shall examine, date, sign, and affix his seal to the summons and thereupon issue and deliver the papers to the appropriate person for service. Affidavits, requests, and any other information relating to the summons and its service as required or permitted by these rules shall be included in a praecipe attached to or entered upon the summons. Such praecipe shall be deemed to be a part of the summons for purposes of these rules. Separate or additional summons shall, as provided by these rules, be issued by the clerk at any time upon proper request of the person seeking service or his attorney.

(C) Form of summons. The summons shall contain:

(1) The name and address of the person on whom the service is to be effected;

(2) The name, street address, and telephone number of the court and the cause number assigned to the case;

(3) The title of the case as shown by the complaint, but, if there are multiple parties, the title may be shortened to include only the first named plaintiff and defendant with an appropriate indication that there are additional parties;

(4) The name, address, and telephone number of the attorney for the person seeking service;

(5) The time within which these rules require the person being served to respond, and a clear statement that in case of his failure to do so, judgment by default may be rendered against him for the relief demanded in the complaint.

The summons may also contain any additional information which will facilitate proper service.

(D) Designation of Manner of Service. The person seeking service or his attorney may designate the manner of service upon the summons. If not so designated, the clerk shall cause service to be made by mail or other public means provided the mailing address of the person to be served is indicated in the summons or can be determined. If a mailing address is not furnished or cannot be determined or if service by mail or other public means is returned without acceptance, the complaint and summons shall promptly be delivered to the sheriff or his deputy who, unless otherwise directed, shall serve the summons.

(E) Summons and Complaint Served Together--Exceptions. The summons and complaint shall be served together unless otherwise ordered by the court. When service of summons is made by publication, the complaint shall not be published. When jurisdiction over a party is dependent upon service of process by publication or by his appearance, summons and complaint shall be deemed to have been served at the end of the day of last required publication in the case of service by publication, and at the time of appearance in jurisdiction acquired by appearance. Whenever the summons and complaint are not served or published together, the summons shall contain the full, unabbreviated title of the case.

(F) Limits of Effective Service. Process may be served anywhere within the state and outside the state as provided in these rules.

Rule 4.1. Summons: Service on individuals

(A) In General. Service may be made upon an individual, or an individual acting in a representative capacity, by:

(1) sending a copy of the summons and complaint by registered or certified mail or other public means by which a written acknowledgment of receipt may be requested and obtained to his residence, place of business or employment with return receipt requested and returned showing receipt of the letter; or

(2) delivering a copy of the summons and complaint to him personally; or

(3) leaving a copy of the summons and complaint at his dwelling house or usual place of abode; or

(4) serving his agent as provided by rule, statute or valid agreement.

(B) Copy Service to Be Followed With Mail. Whenever service is made under Clause (3) or (4) of subdivision (A), the person making the service also shall send by first class mail, a copy of the summons and the complaint to the last known address of the person being served, and this fact shall be shown upon the return.

Rule 4.2. Summons: Service upon infant or incompetents

(A) Service Upon Infants. Service upon an individual known to be an infant shall be made upon his next friend or guardian ad litem, if service is with respect to the same action in which the infant is so represented. If there is no next friend or guardian ad litem, service shall be made upon his court-appointed representative if one is known and can be served within this state. If there is no court-appointed representative, service shall be made upon either parent known to have custody of the infant, or if there is no parent, upon a person known to be standing in the position of custodian or parent. The infant shall also be served if he is fourteen [14] years of age or older. In the event that service, as provided above, is not possible, service shall be made on the infant.

(B) Service Upon Incompetents. Service upon an individual who has been adjudged to be of unsound mind, otherwise incompetent or who is believed to be such shall be made upon his next friend or guardian ad litem, if service is with respect to the same action in which the incompetent is so represented. If there is no next friend or guardian ad litem, service shall be made upon his court-appointed representative if one is known and can be served within this state. If there is no court-appointed representative, then upon the named party and also upon a person known to be standing in the position of custodian of his person.

(C) Duty to Inform Court--Appearance. Nothing herein is intended to affect the duty of a party to inform the court that a person is an infant or incompetent. An appearance by a court-appointed guardian, next friend or guardian ad litem or his attorney shall correct any defect in service under this section unless such defect be challenged.

Rule 4.3. Summons: Service upon institutionalized persons

Service of summons upon a person who is imprisoned or restrained in an institution shall be made by delivering or mailing a copy of the summons and complaint to the official in charge of the institution. It shall be the duty of said official to immediately deliver the summons and complaint to the person being served and allow him to make provisions for adequate representation by counsel. The official shall indicate upon the return whether the person has received the summons and been allowed an opportunity to retain counsel.

Rule 4.4. Service upon persons in actions for acts done in this state or having an effect in this state.

(A) Acts Serving as a Basis for Jurisdiction. Any person or organization that is a nonresident of this state, a resident of this state who has left the state, or a person whose residence is unknown, submits to the jurisdiction of the courts of this state as to any action arising from the following acts committed by him or her or his or her agent:

(1) doing any business in this state;

(2) causing personal injury or property damage by an act or omission done within this state;

(3) causing personal injury or property damage in this state by an occurrence, act or omission done outside this state if he regularly does or solicits business or engages in any other persistent course of conduct, or derives substantial revenue or benefit from goods, materials, or services used, consumed, or rendered in this state;

(4) having supplied or contracted to supply services rendered or to be rendered or goods or materials furnished or to be furnished in this state;

(5) owning, using, or possessing any real property or an interest in real property within this state;

(6) contracting to insure or act as surety for or on behalf of any person, property or risk located within this state at the time the contract was made;

(7) living in the marital relationship within the state notwithstanding subsequent departure from the state, as to all obligations for alimony, custody, child support, or property settlement, if the other party to the marital relationship continues to reside in the state; or

(8) abusing, harassing, or disturbing the peace of, or violating a protective or restraining order for the protection of, any person within the state by an act or omission done in this state, or outside this state if the act or omission is part of a continuing course of conduct having an effect in this state.

In addition, a court of this state may exercise jurisdiction on any basis not inconsistent with the Constitutions of this state or the United States.

(B) Manner of service. A person subject to the jurisdiction of the courts of this state under this rule may be served with summons:

(1) As provided by Rules 4.1 (service on individuals), 4.5 (service upon resident who cannot be found or served within the state), 4.6 (service upon organizations), 4.9 (in rem actions); or

(2) The person shall be deemed to have appointed the Secretary of State as his agent upon whom service of summons may be made as provided in Rule 4.10.

(C) More convenient forum. Jurisdiction under this rule is subject to the power of the court to order the litigation to be held elsewhere under such reasonable conditions as the court in its discretion may determine to be just.

In the exercise of that discretion the court may appropriately consider such factors as:

(1) Amenability to personal jurisdiction in this state and in any alternative forum of the parties to the action;

(2) Convenience to the parties and witnesses of the trial in this state in any alternative forum;

(3) Differences in conflict of law rules applicable in this state and in the alternative forum; or

(4) Any other factors having substantial bearing upon the selection of a convenient, reasonable and fair place of trial.

(D) Forum Non Conveniens--Stay or Dismissal. No stay or dismissal shall be granted due to a finding of forum non conveniens until all properly joined defendants file with the clerk of the court a written stipulation that each defendant will:

(1) submit to the personal jurisdiction of the courts of the other forum; and

(2) waive any defense based on the statute of limitations applicable in the other forum with respect to all causes of action brought by a party to which this subsection applies.

(E) Order on Forum Non Conveniens--Modification. The court may, on motion and notice to the parties, modify an order granting a stay or dismissal under this subsection and take any further action in the proceeding as the interests of justice may require. If the moving party violates a stipulation required by subsection (D), the court shall withdraw the order staying or dismissing the action and proceed as if the order had never been issued. Notwithstanding any other law, the court shall have continuing jurisdiction for the purposes of this subsection.

Rule 4.5. Summons: Service upon resident who cannot be found or served within the state

When the person to be served is a resident of this state who cannot be served personally or by agent in this state and either cannot be found, has concealed his whereabouts or has left the state, summons may be served in the manner provided by Rule 4.9 (summons in in rem actions).

Rule 4.6. Service upon organizations

(A) Persons to be served. Service upon an organization may be made as follows:

(1) In the case of a domestic or foreign organization upon an executive officer thereof, or if there is an agent appointed or deemed by law to have been appointed to receive service, then upon such agent.

(2) In the case of a partnership, upon a general partner thereof.

(3) In the case of a state governmental organization upon the executive officer thereof and also upon the Attorney General.

(4) In the case of a local governmental organization, upon the executive thereof and upon the attorney for the local governmental organization.

(5) When, in subsections (3) and (4) of this subdivision, a governmental representative is named as a party in his individual name or in such name along with his official title, then also upon such representative.

(B) Manner of service. Service under subdivision (A) of this rule shall be made on the proper person in the manner provided by these rules for service upon individuals, but a person seeking service or his attorney shall not knowingly direct service to be made at the person's dwelling house or place of abode, unless such is an address furnished under the requirements of a statute or valid agreement, or unless an affidavit on or attached to the summons states that service in another manner is impractical.

(C) Service at organization's office. When shown upon an affidavit or in the return, that service upon an organization cannot be made as provided in subdivision (A) or (B) of this rule, service may be made by leaving a copy of the summons and complaint at any office of such organization located within this state with the person in charge of such office.

Rule 4.7. Summons: Service upon agent named by statute or agreement

Whenever an agent (other than an agent appointed to receive service for a governmental organization of this state) has been designated by or pursuant to statute or valid agreement to receive service for the person being served, service may be made upon such agent as follows:

(1) If the agent is a governmental organization or officer designated by or pursuant to statute, service shall be made as provided in Rule 4.10.

(2) If the agent is one other than that described above, service shall be made upon him as provided in Rule 4.1 (service upon individuals) or 4.6 (service upon organizations). If service cannot be made upon such agent, because there is no address furnished as required by statute or valid agreement or his whereabouts in this state are unknown, then his principal shall be deemed to have appointed the Secretary of State as a replacement for the agent and service may be made upon the Secretary of State as provided in Rule 4.10.

Rule 4.8. Summons: Service of pleadings or summons on Attorney General

Service of a copy of the summons and complaint or any pleading upon the Attorney General under these rules or any statute shall be made by personal service upon him, a deputy or clerk at his office, or by mail or other public means to him at such office in the manner provided by Rule 4.1(A)(1), and by Rule 4.11 to the extent applicable.

Rule 4.9. Summons: In rem actions

(A) In general. In any action involving a res situated within this state, service may be made as provided in this rule. The court may render a judgment or decree to the extent of its jurisdiction over the res.

(B) Manner of service. Service under this rule may be made as follows:

(1) By service of summons upon a person or his agent pursuant to these rules; or

(2) By service of summons outside this state in a manner provided by Rule 4.1 (service upon individuals) or by publication outside this state in a manner provided by Rule 4.13 (service by publication) or outside this state in any other manner as provided by these rules; or

(3) By service by publication pursuant to Rule 4.13.

Rule 4.10. Summons: Service upon Secretary of State or other governmental agent

(A) [FN1] **In general.** Whenever, under these rules or any statute, service is made upon the Secretary of State or any other governmental organization or officer, as agent for the person being served, service may be made upon such agent as provided in this rule.

(1) The person seeking service or his attorney shall:

(a) submit his request for service upon the agent in the praecipe for summons, and state that the governmental organization or officer is the agent of the person being served;

(b) state the address of the person being served as filed and recorded pursuant to a statute or valid agreement, or if no such address is known, then his last known mailing address, and, if no such address is known, then such shall be stated;

(c) pay any fee prescribed by statute to be forwarded together with sufficient copies of the summons, affidavit and complaint, to the agent by the clerk of the court.

(2) Upon receipt thereof the agent shall promptly:

(a) send to the person being served a copy of the summons and complaint by registered or certified mail or by other public means by which a written acknowledgment of receipt may be obtained;

(b) complete and deliver to the clerk an affidavit showing the date of the mailing, or if there was no mailing, the reason therefor;

(c) send to the clerk a copy of the return receipt along with a copy of the summons;

(d) file and retain a copy of the return receipt.

[FN1] This rule contains no Subd. (B).

Rule 4.11. Summons: Registered or certified mail

Whenever service by registered or certified mail or other public means by which a return receipt may be requested is authorized, the clerk of the court or a governmental agent under Rule 4.10 shall send the summons and complaint to the person being served at the address supplied upon the summons, or furnished by the person seeking service. In his return the clerk of the court or the governmental agent shall show the date and place of mailing, a copy of the mailed or electronically-transmitted return receipt if and when received by him showing whether the mailing was accepted or returned, and, if accepted, by whom. The return along with the receipt shall be promptly filed by the clerk with the pleadings and become a part of the record. If a mailing by the clerk of the court is returned without acceptance, the clerk shall reissue the summons and complaint for service as requested, by the person seeking service.

Rule 4.12. Summons: Service by sheriff or other officer

(A) In general. Whenever service is made by delivering a copy to a person personally or by leaving a copy at his dwelling house or place of employment as provided by Rule 4.1, summons shall be issued to and served by the sheriff, his deputy, or some person specially or regularly appointed by the court for that purpose. Service shall be effective if made by a person not otherwise authorized by these rules, but proof of service by such a person must be made by him as a witness or by deposition without allowance of expenses therefor as costs. The person to whom the summons is delivered for service must act promptly and exercise reasonable care to cause service to be made.

(B) Special service by police officers. A sheriff, his deputy, or any full-time state or municipal police officer may serve summons in any county of this state if he agrees or has agreed to make the service. When specially requested in the praecipe for summons, the complaint and summons shall be delivered to such officer by the clerk or the attorney for the person seeking service. No agreement with the sheriff or his deputy for such service in the sheriff's own county shall be permitted. In no event shall any expenses agreed upon under this provision be assessed or recovered as costs or affect court costs otherwise imposed for regular service.

(C) Service in other counties. A summons may be served in any county in this state. If service is to be made in another county, the summons may be issued by the clerk for service therein to the sheriff of such county or to a person authorized to make service by these rules.

(D) Service outside the state. Personal service, when permitted by these rules to be made outside the state, may be made there by any disinterested person or by the attorney representing the person seeking such service. The expenses of such person may be assessed as costs only if they are reasonable and if service by mail or other public means cannot be made or is not successful.

Rule 4.13. Summons: Service by publication

(A) Praecipe for summons by publication. In any action where notice by publication is permitted by these rules or by statute, service may be made by publication. Summons by publication may name all the persons to be served, and separate publications with respect to each party shall not be required. The person seeking such service, or his attorney, shall submit his request therefor upon the praecipe for summons along with supporting affidavits that diligent search has been made that the defendant cannot be found, has concealed his whereabouts, or has left the state, and shall prepare the contents of the summons to be published. The summons shall be signed by the clerk of the court or the sheriff in such manner as to indicate that it is made by his authority.

(B) Contents of summons by publication. The summons shall contain the following information:

(1) The name of the person being sued, and the person to whom the notice is directed, and, if the person's whereabouts are unknown or some or all of the parties are unknown, a statement to that effect;

(2) The name of the court and cause number assigned to the case;

(3) The title of the case as shown by the complaint, but if there are multiple parties, the title may be shortened to include only the first named plaintiff and those defendants to be served by publication with an appropriate indication that there are additional parties;

(4) The name and address of the attorney representing the person seeking service;

(5) A brief statement of the nature of the suit, which need not contain the details and particulars of the claim. A description of any property, relationship, or other res involved in the action, and a statement that the person being sued claims some interest therein;

(6) A clear statement that the person being sued must respond within thirty [30] days after the last notice of the action is published, and in case he fails to do so, judgment by default may be entered against him for the relief demanded in the complaint.

(C) Publication of summons. The summons shall be published three [3] times by the clerk or person making it, the first publication promptly and each two [2] succeeding publications at least seven [7] and not more than fourteen [14] days after the prior publication, in a newspaper authorized by law to publish notices, and published in the county where the complaint or action is filed, where the res is located, or where the defendant resides or where he was known last to reside. If no newspaper is published in the county, then the summons shall be published in the county in this state nearest thereto in which any such paper may be printed, or in a place specially ordered by the court. The person seeking the service or his attorney may designate any qualified newspaper, and if he fails to do so, the selection may be made by the clerk.

(D) By whom made or procured. Service of summons by publication shall be made and procured by the clerk, by a person appointed by the court for that purpose, or by the clerk or sheriff of another county where publication is to be made.

(E) Return. The clerk or person making the service shall prepare the return and include the following:

(1) Any supporting affidavits of the printer containing a copy of the summons which was published;

(2) An information or statement that the newspaper and the publication meet all legal requirements applicable to such publication;

(3) The dates of publication.

The return and affidavits shall be filed with the pleadings and other papers in the case and shall become a part of the record as provided in these rules.

Rule 4.14. Service Under Special Order of Court

Upon application of any party the court in which any action is pending may make an appropriate order for service in a manner not provided by these rules or statutes when such service is reasonably calculated to give the defendant actual knowledge of the proceedings and an opportunity to be heard.

Rule 4.15. Summons: Proof of Service--Return--Amendments--Defects

(A) Return--Form. The person making service shall promptly make his return upon or attach it to a copy of the summons which shall be delivered to the clerk. The return shall be signed by the person making it, and shall include a statement:

(1) that service was made upon the person as required by law and the time, place, and manner thereof;

(2) if service was not made, the particular manner in which it was thwarted in terms of fact or in terms of law;

(3) such other information as is expressly required by these rules.

(B) Return and affidavits as evidence. The return, along with the summons to which it is attached or is a part, the praecipe for summons, affidavits furnished with the summons or praecipe for summons, and all other affidavits permitted by these rules shall be filed by the clerk with the pleadings and other papers in the case and thereupon shall become a part of the record, and have such evidentiary effect as is now provided by law. Copies of such record shall be admissible in all actions and proceedings and may be entered in any public records when certified over the signature of the clerk or his deputy and the clerk's seal.

(C) Proof of filing and issuance dates. The clerk shall enter a filing date upon every praecipe, pleading, return, summons, affidavit or other paper filed with or entered of record by him. The clerk shall also enter an issuance date upon any summons issued, mailed or delivered by him, or other communication served or transmitted by him under these rules. Such filing or issuance date shall constitute evidence of the date of filing or issuance without further authentication when entered in the court records, or when the paper or a copy thereof is otherwise properly offered or admitted into evidence.

(D) Admission of service. A written admission stating the date and place of service, signed by the person being served, may be filed with the clerk who shall file it with the pleadings. Such admission shall become a part of the record, constitute evidence of proper service, and shall be allowed as evidence in any action or proceeding.

(E) Amendment. At any time in its discretion and upon such terms as it deems just, the court may allow any process or proof of service thereof to be amended unless it clearly appears that material prejudice would result to the substantial rights of the person against whom the process is issued.

(F) Defects in summons. No summons or the service thereof shall be set aside or be adjudged insufficient when either is reasonably calculated to inform the person to be served that an action has been instituted against him, the name of the court, and the time within which he is required to respond.

Rule 4.16. Summons: Duties of persons to aid in service

(A) It shall be the duty of every person being served under these rules to cooperate, accept service, comply with the provisions of these rules, and, when service is made upon him personally, acknowledge receipt of the papers in writing over his signature.

(1) Offering or tendering the papers to the person being served and advising the person that he or she is being served is adequate service.

(2) A person who has refused to accept the offer or tender of the papers being served thereafter may not challenge the service of those papers.

(B) Anyone accepting service for another person is under a duty to:

(1) promptly deliver the papers to that person;

(2) promptly notify that person that he holds the papers for him; or

(3) within a reasonable time, in writing, notify the clerk or person making the service that he has been unable to make such delivery of notice when such is the case.

(C) No person through whom service is made under these rules may impose any sanction, penalty, punishment, or discrimination whatsoever against the person being served because of such service. Any person willfully violating any provision of this rule may be subjected to contempt proceedings.

Rule 4.17. Summons: Certain proceedings excepted

Rules 4 through 4.16 shall not replace the manner of serving summons or giving notice as specially provided by statute or rule in proceedings involving, without limitation, the administration of decedent's estates, guardianships, receiverships, or assignments for the benefit of creditors.

Rule 5. Service and Filing of Pleading and Other Papers

(A) Service: When Required. Unless otherwise provided by these rules or an order of the court, each party and special judge, if any, shall be served with:

(1) every order required by its terms to be served;

(2) every pleading subsequent to the original complaint;

(3) every written motion except one which may be heard ex parte;

(4) every brief submitted to the trial court;

(5) every paper relating to discovery required to be served upon a party; and

(6) every written notice, appearance, demand, offer of judgment, designation of record on appeal, or similar paper.

No service need be made on parties in default for failure to appear, except that pleadings asserting new or additional claims for relief against them shall be served upon them in the manner provided by service of summons in Rule 4.

(B) Service: How made. Whenever a party is represented by an attorney of record, service shall be made upon such attorney unless service upon the party is ordered by the court. Service upon the attorney or party shall be made by delivering or mailing a copy of the papers to the last known address, or where service is by FAX or e-mail, by faxing or e-mailing a copy of the documents to the fax number or e-mail address set out in the appearance form or correction as required by Rule 3.1(E).

(1) Delivery. Delivery of a copy within this rule means

(a) offering or tendering it to the attorney or party and stating the nature of the papers being served. Refusal to accept an offered or tendered document is a waiver of any objection to the sufficiency or adequacy of service of that document;

(b) leaving it at his office with a clerk or other person in charge thereof, or if there is no one in charge, leaving it in a conspicuous place therein; or

(c) if the office is closed, by leaving it at his dwelling house or usual place of abode with some person of suitable age and discretion then residing therein; or,

(d) leaving it at some other suitable place, selected by the attorney upon whom service is being made, pursuant to duly promulgated local rule.

(2) *Service by Mail.* If service is made by mail, the papers shall be deposited in the United States mail addressed to the person on whom they are being served, with postage prepaid. Service shall be deemed complete upon mailing. Proof of service of all papers permitted to be mailed may be made by written acknowledgment of service, by affidavit of the person who mailed the papers, or by certificate of an attorney. It shall be the duty of attorneys when entering their appearance in a cause or when filing pleadings or papers therein, to have noted in the Chronological Case Summary or said pleadings or papers so filed the address and telephone number of their office. Service by delivery or by mail at such address shall be deemed sufficient and complete.

(3) *Service by FAX or e-mail.*

(a) Service by e-mail from the Clerk. The Clerk may transmit notice of all rulings, orders, or judgments required by Trial Rule 72(D) by e-mail to all parties represented by attorneys and to all unrepresented parties who have supplied the Court with an e-mail address for service. Where a copy of a written ruling, order, or judgment is being transmitted by e-mail, service may be made by including a link to the document or by attaching the document being served to the e-mail in .pdf format.

(b) Service by FAX or e-mail from other parties. A party who has consented to service by FAX or e-mail may be served by attaching the document being served to an e-mail in .pdf format. Discovery documents must also be served in accordance with Trial Rule 26(A).

(c) Completion of service by FAX or email. Service by FAX or e-mail shall be deemed complete upon transmission. Service that occurs on a Saturday, Sunday, a legal holiday, or a day the court or agency in which the matter is pending is closed, or after 5:00 p.m. local time of the recipient shall be deemed complete the next day that is not a Saturday, Sunday, a legal holiday, or a day the court or agency in which the matter is pending is not closed.

(C) Certificate of Service. An attorney or unrepresented party tendering a document to the Clerk for filing shall certify that service has been made, list the parties served, and specify the date and means of service. The certificate of service shall be placed at the end of the document and shall not be separately filed. The separate filing of a certificate of service, however, shall not be grounds for rejecting a document for filing. The Clerk may permit documents to be filed without a certificate of service but shall require prompt filing of a separate certificate of service.

(D) Same: Numerous defendants. In any action in which there are unusually large numbers of defendants, the court, upon motion or of its own initiative, may order

(1) that service of the pleadings of the defendants and replies thereto need not be made as between the defendants;

(2) that any cross-claim, counterclaim, or matter constituting an avoidance or affirmative defense contained therein shall be deemed to be denied or avoided by all other parties; and

(3) that the filing of any such pleading and service thereof upon the plaintiff constitutes due notice of it to the parties.

A copy of every such order shall be served upon the parties in such manner and form as the court directs.

(E) Filing.

(1) Except as otherwise provided in subparagraph (2) hereof, all pleadings and papers subsequent to the complaint which are required to be served upon a party shall be filed with the Court either before service or within a reasonable period of time thereafter.

(2) No deposition or request for discovery or response thereto under Trial Rules 27, 30, 31, 33, 34 or 36 shall be filed with the Court unless:

(a) A motion is filed pursuant to Trial Rule 26(C) or Trial Rule 37 and the original deposition or request for discovery or response thereto is necessary to enable the Court to rule; or

(b) A party desires to use the deposition or request for discovery or response thereto for evidentiary purposes at trial or in connection with a motion, and the Court, either upon its own motion or that of any party, or as a part of any pre-trial order, orders the filing of the original.

(3) Custody of original and Period of Retention:

(a) The original of a deposition shall, subject to the provisions of Trial Rule 30(E), be delivered by the reporter to the party taking it and shall be maintained by that party until filed with the Court pursuant to paragraph (2) or until the later of final judgment, agreed settlement of the litigation or all appellate rights have been exhausted.

(b) The original or any request for discovery or response thereto under Trial Rules 27, 30, 31, 33, 34 and 36 shall be maintained by the party originating the request or response until filed with the Court pursuant to paragraph (2) or until the later of final judgment, agreed settlement or all appellate rights have been exhausted.

(4) In the event it is made to appear to the satisfaction of the Court that the original of a deposition or request for discovery or response thereto cannot be filed with the Court when required, the Court may allow use of a copy instead of the original.

(5) The filing of any deposition shall constitute publication.

(F) Filing With the Court Defined. The filing of pleadings, motions, and other papers with the court as required by these rules shall be made by one of the following methods:

(1) Delivery to the clerk of the court;

(2) Sending by electronic transmission under the procedure adopted pursuant to Administrative Rule 12;

(3) Mailing to the clerk by registered, certified or express mail return receipt requested;

(4) Depositing with any third-party commercial carrier for delivery to the clerk within three (3) calendar days, cost prepaid, properly addressed;

(5) If the court so permits, filing with the judge, in which event the judge shall note thereon the filing date and forthwith transmit them to the office of the clerk; or

(6) Electronic filing, as approved by the Indiana Office of Judicial Administration (IOJA) pursuant to Administrative Rule 16.

Filing by registered or certified mail and by third-party commercial carrier shall be complete upon mailing or deposit

Any party filing any paper by any method other than personal delivery to the clerk shall retain proof of filing.

(G) Confidentiality of Court Records.

(1) Court Records are accessible to the public, except as provided in Administrative Rule 9(G).

(2) Any Court Record excluded from Public Access pursuant to Administrative Rule 9(G) must be filed in accordance with Administrative Rule 9(G)(5).

(H) Distribution of Orders.

(1) Unless otherwise provided by statute or these rules, the clerk shall distribute signed orders to non-defaulting parties for whom an e-mail address has not been provided.

(2) All orders in Trial Rule 69 Proceedings Supplemental, Execution, and Foreclosure Sales shall be distributed for service by the party who submitted the proposed order.

Rule 6. Time

(A) Computation. In computing any period of time prescribed or allowed by these rules, by order of the court, or by any applicable statute, the day of the act, event, or default from which the designated period of time begins to run shall not be included. The last day of the period so computed is to be included unless it is:

(1) a Saturday,

(2) a Sunday,

(3) a legal holiday as defined by state statute, or

(4) a day the office in which the act is to be done is closed during regular business hours.

In any event, the period runs until the end of the next day that is not a Saturday, a Sunday, a legal holiday, or a day on which the office is closed. When the period of time allowed is less than seven [7] days, intermediate Saturdays, Sundays, legal holidays, and days on which the office is closed shall be excluded from the computations.

(B) Enlargement. When an act is required or allowed to be done at or within a specific time by these rules, the court may at any time for cause shown:

(1) order the period enlarged, with or without motion or notice, if request therefor is made before the expiration of the period originally prescribed or extended by a previous order; or

(2) upon motion made after the expiration of the specific period, permit the act to be done where the failure to act was the result of excusable neglect; but, the court may not extend the time for taking any action for judgment on the evidence under Rule 50(A), amendment of findings and judgment under Rule 52(B), to correct errors under Rule 59(C), statement in opposition to motion to correct error under Rule 59(E), or to obtain relief from final judgment under Rule 60(B), except to the extent and under the conditions stated in those rules.

(C) Service of pleadings and Rule 12 motions. A responsive pleading required under these rules, shall be served within twenty [20] days after service of the prior pleading. Unless the court specifies otherwise, a reply shall be served within twenty [20] days after entry of an order requiring it. The service of a motion permitted under Rule 12 alters the time for service of responsive pleadings as follows, unless a different time is fixed by the court:

(1) if the court does not grant the motion, the responsive pleading shall be served in ten [10] days after notice of the court's action;

(2) if the court grants the motion and the corrective action is allowed to be taken, it shall be taken within ten [10] days, and the responsive pleading shall be served within ten [10] days thereafter.

(D) For motions--Affidavits. A written motion, other than one which may be heard ex parte, and notice of the hearing thereof shall be served not less than five [5] days before the time specified for the hearing, unless a different period is fixed by these rules or by order of the court. Such an order may, for cause shown, be made on ex parte application. When a motion is supported by affidavit, the affidavit shall be served with the motion; and except as otherwise provided in Rule 59(D), opposing affidavits may be served not less than one [1] day before the hearing, unless the court permits them to be served at some other time.

(E) Additional time after service by United States mail. Whenever a party has the right or is required to do some act or take some proceedings within a prescribed period after the service of a notice or other paper upon him and the notice or paper is served upon him by United States mail, three [3] days shall be added to the prescribed period.

(F) Dissolution Actions--Sixty-day waiting period. No cause for dissolution of marriage or for legal separation shall be tried or heard by any court until after the expiration of sixty (60) days from the date of the filing of the petition or from the date of the publication of the first notice to a nonresident.

Rule 7. Pleadings allowed--Form of motion

(A) Pleadings. The pleadings shall consist of:

(1) a complaint and an answer;

(2) a reply to a denominated counterclaim;

(3) an answer to a cross-claim;

(4) a third-party complaint, if a person not an original party is summoned under the provisions of Rule 14; and

(5) a third-party answer.

No other pleadings shall be allowed; but the court may, in its discretion, order a reply to an answer or third-party answer. Matters formerly required to be pleaded by a reply or other subsequent pleading may be proved even though they are not pleaded.

(B) Motions and other papers. Unless made during a hearing or trial, or otherwise ordered by the court, an application to the court for an order shall be made by written motion. The motion shall state the grounds therefor and the relief or order sought. The requirement of notice is satisfied by service of the motion.

(C) Demurrers, pleas, etc., abolished. Demurrers, pleas in abatement, and exceptions for insufficiency of a pleading or improper service shall not be used. All objections and defenses formerly raised by such motions shall now be raised pursuant to Rule 12.

Rule 8. General rules of pleading

(A) Claims for Relief. To state a claim for relief, whether an original claim, counterclaim, cross-claim, or third-party claim, a pleading must contain:

(1) a short and plain statement of the claim showing that the pleader is entitled to relief, and

(2) a demand for relief to which the pleader deems entitled. Relief in the alternative or of several different types may be demanded. However, in any complaint seeking damages for personal injury or death, or seeking punitive damages, no dollar amount or figure shall be included in the demand.

(B) Defenses: Form of denials. A responsive pleading shall state in short and plain terms the pleader's defenses to each claim asserted and shall admit or controvert the averments set forth in the preceding pleading. If in good faith the pleader intends to deny all the averments in the preceding pleading, he may do so by general denial subject to the provisions of Rule 11. If he does not intend a general denial, he may:

(1) specifically deny designated averments or paragraphs; or

(2) generally deny all averments except such designated averments and paragraphs as he expressly admits.

If he lacks knowledge or information sufficient to form a belief as to the truth of an averment, he shall so state and his statement shall be considered a denial. If in good faith a pleader intends to deny only a part or a qualification of an averment, he shall specify so much of it as is true and material and deny the remainder. All denials shall fairly meet the substance of the averments denied. This rule shall have no application to uncontested actions for divorce, or to answers required to be filed by clerks or guardians ad litem.

(C) Affirmative defenses. A responsive pleading shall set forth affirmatively and carry the burden of proving: accord and satisfaction, arbitration and award, discharge in bankruptcy, duress, estoppel, failure of consideration, fraud, illegality, injury by fellow servant, laches, license, payment, release, res judicata, statute of frauds, statute of limitations, waiver, lack of jurisdiction over the subject-matter, lack of jurisdiction over the person, improper venue, insufficiency of process or service of process, the same action pending in another state court of this state, and any other matter constituting an avoidance, matter of abatement, or affirmative defense. A party required to affirmatively plead any matters, including matters formerly required to be pleaded affirmatively by reply, shall have the burden of proving such matters. The burden of proof imposed by this or any other provision of these rules is subject to the rules of evidence or any statute fixing a different rule. If the pleading mistakenly designates a defense as a counterclaim or a counterclaim as a defense, the court shall treat the pleading as if there had been a proper designation.

(D) Effect of failure to deny. Averments in a pleading to which a responsive pleading is required, except those pertaining to amount of damages, are admitted when not denied in the responsive pleading. Averments in a pleading to which no responsive pleading is required or permitted shall be taken as denied or avoided.

(E) All pleadings to be concise and direct--Consistency.

(1) Each averment of a pleading shall be simple, concise, and direct. No technical forms of pleading or motions are required. All fictions in pleading are abolished.

(2) A pleading may set forth two [2] or more statements of a claim or defense alternatively or hypothetically, either in one [1] count or defense or in separate counts or defenses. When two [2] or more statements are made in the alternative and one [1] of them if made independently would be sufficient, the pleading is not made insufficient by the insufficiency of one or more of the alternative statements. A pleading may also state as many separate claims or defenses as the pleader has regardless of consistency and whether based on legal or equitable grounds. All statements shall be made subject to the obligations set forth in Rule 11.

(3) Motions and pleadings, joint and several. All motions and pleadings of any kind addressed to two [2] or more paragraphs of any pleading, or filed by two [2] or more parties, shall be taken and construed as joint, separate, and several motions or pleadings to each of such paragraphs and by and against each of such parties. All motions or pleadings containing two [2] or more subject-matters shall be taken and construed as separate and several as to each subject-matter. All objections to rulings made by two [2] or more parties shall be taken and construed as the joint, separate, and several objections of each of such parties.

A complaint filed by or against two [2] or more plaintiffs shall be taken and construed as joint, separate, and several as to each of said plaintiffs.

(F) Construction of pleadings. All pleadings shall be so construed as to do substantial justice, lead to disposition on the merits, and avoid litigation of procedural points.

Rule 9. Pleading special matters

(A) Capacity. It is not necessary to aver the capacity of a party to sue or be sued, the authority of a party to sue or be sued in a representative capacity, or the legal existence of an organization that is made a party. The burden of proving lack of such capacity, authority, or legal existence shall be upon the person asserting lack of it, and shall be pleaded as an affirmative defense.

(B) Fraud, mistake, condition of the mind. In all averments of fraud or mistake, the circumstances constituting fraud or mistake shall be specifically averred. Malice, intent, knowledge, and other conditions of mind may be averred generally.

(C) Conditions precedent. In pleading the performance or occurrence of promissory or non-promissory conditions precedent, it is sufficient to aver generally that all conditions precedent have been performed, have occurred, or have been excused. A denial of performance or occurrence shall be made specifically and with particularity, and a denial of excuse generally.

(D) Official document or act. In pleading an official document or official act it is sufficient to aver that the document was issued or the act done in compliance with law.

(E) Judgment. In pleading a judgment or decision of a domestic or foreign court, judicial or quasi-judicial tribunal, or of a board or officer, it is sufficient to aver the judgment or decision without setting forth matter showing jurisdiction to render it.

(F) Time and place. For the purpose of testing the sufficiency of a pleading, averments of time and place are material and shall be considered like all other averments of material matter. However, time and place need be stated only with such specificity as will enable the opposing party to prepare his defense.

(G) Special damages--Damages where no answer. When items of special damage are claimed, they shall be specifically stated. The relief granted to the plaintiff, if there be no answer, cannot exceed the relief demanded in his complaint; but, in any other case, the court may grant him any relief consistent with the facts or matters pleaded.

Rule 9.1. Pleading and proof of contributory negligence, assumed risk, res ipsa loquitur, consideration, bona fide purchaser, matters of judicial notice--Answer of distraint

(A) **Defense of contributory negligence or assumed risk.** In all claims alleging negligence, the burden of pleading and proving contributory negligence, assumption of risk, or incurred risk shall be upon the defendant who may plead such by denial of the allegation.

(B) **Res ipsa loquitur.** Res ipsa loquitur or a similar doctrine may be pleaded by alleging generally that the facts connected with the action are unknown to the pleader and are within the knowledge of the opposing party.

(C) **Consideration.** When an action or defense is founded upon a written contract or release, lack of consideration for the promise or release is an affirmative defense, and the party asserting lack of it carries the burden of proof.

(D) **Bona fide purchaser.** When the rights of a person depend upon his status as a bona fide purchaser for value or upon similar requirements, such status must be pleaded and proved by the person asserting it, but it may be pleaded in general terms. Once it is established that the person has given any required value, unless such value is commercially unreasonable, and that he has met any requirements of recordation, filing, possession, or perfection, the trier of fact must find that such value was given or such perfection was made in accordance with any requirements of good faith, lack of knowledge, or lack of notice unless and until evidence is introduced which would support a finding of its non-existence.

(E) **Presumption--Matters of judicial notice.** Neither presumptions of law nor matters of which judicial notice may be taken need be stated in a pleading.

(F) **Property distrained--Sufficient answer.** In an action to recover the possession of property distrained while doing damage, an answer that the defendant, or person by whose command he acted, was lawfully possessed of the real property upon which the distress was made, and that the property distrained was at the time doing damage thereon, shall be good without setting forth the title of such real property.

Rule 9.2. Pleading and proof of written instruments

(A) **When instrument or copy, or an Affidavit of Debt must be filed.** When any pleading allowed by these rules is founded on a written instrument, the original, or a copy thereof, must be included in or filed with the pleading. Such instrument, whether copied in the pleadings or not, shall be taken as part of the record.

When any pleading allowed by these rules is founded on an account, an Affidavit of Debt in a form substantially similar to that which is provided in Appendix A-2 to these rules, shall be attached.

(B) **Proof of execution of instruments filed with pleadings.** When a pleading is founded on a written instrument and the instrument or a copy thereof is included in or filed with the pleading, execution of such instrument, indorsement, or assignment shall be deemed to be established and the instrument, if otherwise admissible, shall be deemed admitted into evidence in the action without proving its execution unless execution be denied under oath in the responsive pleading or by an affidavit filed therewith. A denial asserting that another person who is not a party did execute the instrument, indorsement, or assignment may be made without such oath or affidavit only if the pleader alleges under oath or in an accompanying affidavit that after the exercise of reasonable diligence he was unable to make such person or his representative (subdivision (H)) a party, the reason therefor, and that he is without information as to such execution.

(C) **Oath or affidavit of denial of execution must be made upon personal knowledge.** An oath or affidavit denying execution as required and made under subdivision (B) of this rule shall be made upon the personal knowledge of the person making it, and, if general in form (Rule 11(B)), shall be deemed to be made upon such personal knowledge.

(D) **Burden of proving execution.** The ultimate burden of proving the execution of a written instrument is upon the party claiming its validity, but execution is presumed. "Presumed" means that the trier of fact must find the existence of the fact presumed unless and until evidence is introduced which would support a finding of its nonexistence.

(E) **Inspection of the original instrument.** When a copy of a written instrument is filed with or copied in the pleadings under the provisions of this rule, the pleader shall permit inspection of the original unless it is alleged that the original is lost, whether by destruction, theft or otherwise, or unless it is alleged or established that the instrument is in the possession of another person and out of the control of the pleader or that the duty to allow inspection is otherwise excused. The pleader shall allow inspection promptly upon request of a party, and inspection may be ordered by the court upon motion without a hearing at any time. A party failing to comply with such request or such order shall be subject to the provisions of Rule 37(B). This provision shall not diminish a party's rights under Rules 26 through 38.

(F) **Effect of non-compliance--Amendments.** Non-compliance with the provisions of this rule requiring a written instrument or an Affidavit of Debt to be included with the pleading may be raised by the first responsive pleading or prior motion of a party. The court, in its sound discretion, may order compliance, the reasons for non-compliance to be added to the pleadings, or allow the action to continue without further pleading. Amendments to correct the omission of a required written instrument, an assignment or indorsement thereof, the omission of a denial of the execution of a written instrument as permitted or required by this rule, or an Affidavit of Debt shall be governed by Rule 15, except as provided by subdivision (A) of this rule.

(G) Exceptions--Infants, incompetents, dead and insolvent persons. The requirement of this rule that execution of a written instrument be denied under oath or otherwise, shall not apply against a party who is not required to file a responsive pleading, or against a party who, at the time the responsive pleading is due or before the pleadings are closed, is or becomes dead, an infant or adjudicated incompetent or is the representative of such person or of a person who is dead, an infant, an adjudicated incompetent, or in insolvency proceedings. Such parties shall be deemed to have denied execution or admissibility without any responsive pleading or denial. The presumption of execution as provided in subdivision (D) of this rule shall not apply to establish execution of a written instrument by a person who, at the time proof is required, is dead, an infant or adjudicated incompetent.

(H) "Execution" of a written instrument. "Execution" of a written instrument includes the following requirements:

(1) That a signature was made with express, implied or apparent authority and was not forged;

(2) That the instrument was properly delivered, including any requisite intent that it be effective;

(3) That the written terms of the instrument have not been materially altered without the express, implied or apparent authority of the person bound thereon;

(4) That the person seeking its enforcement is in possession of the instrument when required; and

(5) That the names or identity of the persons named in the instrument are correct.

(I) "Written instrument": When pleading is founded thereon--When pleading is not founded thereon term includes documents. When a pleading is founded upon a written instrument, any written indorsement or assignment of rights thereof upon which the pleader's title depends is included in the term "written instrument."

Rule 10. Form of pleading

(A) Caption--Names of parties. Every pleading shall contain a caption setting forth the name of the court, the title of the action, the file number, and a designation as in Rule 7(A). In the complaint the title of the action shall include the names of all the parties, but in other pleadings it is sufficient to state the name of the first party on each side with an appropriate indication of other parties.

(B) Paragraphs--Separate statements. All averments of a claim or defense shall be made in numbered paragraphs, the contents of each of which shall be limited as far as practicable to a statement of a single set of circumstances, and a paragraph may be referred to by number in all succeeding pleadings. Each claim founded upon a separate transaction or occurrence and each defense other than denials may be stated in a separate count or defense whenever a separation facilitates the clear presentation of the matters set forth.

(C) Adoption by reference--Exhibits. Statements in a pleading may be adopted by reference in a different part of the same pleading or in another pleading or in any motion. A copy of any written instrument which is an exhibit to a pleading is a part thereof for all purposes.

Rule 11. Signing and verification of pleadings

(A) Parties Represented by Attorney. Every pleading or motion of a party represented by an attorney shall be signed by at least one [1] attorney of record in his individual name, whose address, telephone number, and attorney number shall be stated, except that this provision shall not apply to pleadings and motions made and transcribed at the trial or a hearing before the judge and received by him in such form. A party who is not represented by an attorney shall sign his pleading and state his address. Except when specifically required by rule, pleadings or motions need not be verified or accompanied by affidavit. The rule in equity that the averments of an answer under oath must be overcome by the testimony of two [2] witnesses or of one [1] witness sustained by corroborating circumstances is abolished. The signature of an attorney constitutes a certificate by him that he has read the pleadings; that to the best of his knowledge, information, and belief, there is good ground to support it; and that it is not interposed for delay. If a pleading or motion is not signed or is signed with intent to defeat the purpose of the rule, it may be stricken as sham and false and the action may proceed as though the pleading had not been served. For a willful violation of this rule an attorney may be subjected to appropriate disciplinary action. Similar action may be taken if scandalous or indecent matter is inserted.

(B) Verification by affirmation or representation. When in connection with any civil or special statutory proceeding it is required that any pleading, motion, petition, supporting affidavit, or other document of any kind, be verified, or that an oath be taken, it shall be sufficient if the subscriber simply affirms the truth of the matter to be verified by an affirmation or representation in substantially the following language:

"I (we) affirm, under the penalties for perjury, that the foregoing representation(s) is (are) true.

(Signed) ______________"

Any person who falsifies an affirmation or representation of fact shall be subject to the same penalties as are prescribed by law for the making of a false affidavit.

(C) Verified pleadings, motions, and affidavits as evidence. Pleadings, motions and affidavits accompanying or in support of such pleadings or motions when required to be verified or under oath shall be accepted as a representation that the signer had personal knowledge thereof or reasonable cause to believe the existence of the facts or matters stated or alleged therein; and, if otherwise competent or acceptable as evidence may be admitted as evidence of the facts or matters stated or alleged therein when it is so provided in these rules, by statute or other law, or to the extent the writing or signature expressly purports to be made upon the signer's personal knowledge. When such pleadings, motions and affidavits are verified or under oath they shall not require other or greater proof on the part of the adverse party than if not verified or not under oath unless expressly provided otherwise by these rules, statute or other law. Affidavits upon motions for summary judgment under Rule 56 and in denial of execution under Rule 9.2 shall be made upon personal knowledge.

Rule 12. Defenses and objections -- When and how presented -- By pleading or motion -- Motion for judgment on the pleadings

(A) When presented. The time allowed for the presentation of defenses and objections in a motion or responsive pleading shall be computed pursuant to the provisions of Rule 6(C).

(B) How presented. Every defense, in law or fact, to a claim for relief in any pleading, whether a claim, counterclaim, cross-claim, or third-party claim, shall be asserted in the responsive pleading thereto if one is required; except that at the option of the pleader, the following defenses may be made by motion:

(1) Lack of jurisdiction over the subject matter,

(2) Lack of jurisdiction over the person,

(3) Incorrect venue under Trial Rule 75, or any statutory provision. The disposition of this motion shall be consistent with Trial Rule 75,

(4) Insufficiency of process;

(5) Insufficiency of service of process;

(6) Failure to state a claim upon which relief can be granted, which shall include failure to name the real party in interest under Rule 17;

(7) Failure to join a party needed for just adjudication under Rule 19;

(8) The same action pending in another state court of this state.

A motion making any of these defenses shall be made before pleading if a further pleading is permitted or within twenty [20] days after service of the prior pleading if none is required. If a pleading sets forth a claim for relief to which the adverse party is not required to serve a responsive pleading, any of the defenses in section (B)(2), (3), (4), (5) or (8) is waived to the extent constitutionally permissible unless made in a motion within twenty [20] days after service of the prior pleading. No defense or objection is waived by being joined with one or more other defenses or objections in a responsive pleading or motion.

When a motion to dismiss is sustained for failure to state a claim under subdivision (B)(6) of this rule the pleading may be amended once as of right pursuant to Rule 15(A) within ten [10] days after service of notice of the court's order sustaining the motion and thereafter with permission of the court pursuant to such rule.

If, on a motion, asserting the defense number (6), to dismiss for failure of the pleading to state a claim upon which relief can be granted, matters outside the pleading are presented to and not excluded by the court, the motion shall be treated as one for summary judgment and disposed of as provided in Rule 56. In such case, all parties shall be given reasonable opportunity to present all material made pertinent to such a motion by Rule 56.

(C) Motion for judgment on the pleadings. After the pleadings are closed but within such time as not to delay the trial, any party may move for judgment on the pleadings. If, on a motion for judgment on the pleadings, matters outside the pleadings are presented to and not excluded by the court, the motion shall be treated as one for summary judgment and disposed of as provided in Rule 56, and all parties shall be given reasonable opportunity to present all material made pertinent to such a motion by Rule 56.

(D) Preliminary determination. Whether made in a pleading or by motion, the defenses specifically enumerated (1) to (8) in subdivision (B) of this rule, and the motion for judgment on the pleadings mentioned in subdivision (C) of this rule shall, upon application of any party or by order of court, be determined before trial unless substantial justice requires the court to defer hearing until trial.

(E) Motion for more definite statement. If a pleading to which a responsive pleading is permitted is so vague or ambiguous that a party cannot reasonably be required to frame a responsive pleading, he may move for a more definite statement before interposing his responsive pleading. The motion shall point out the defects complained of and the details desired. If the motion is granted and the order of the court is not obeyed within twenty [20] days after notice of the order or within such other time as the court may fix, the court may strike the pleading to which the motion was directed or make such order as it deems just.

(F) Motion to strike. Upon motion made by a party before responding to a pleading, or, if no responsive pleading is permitted by these rules, upon motion made by a party within twenty [20] days after the service of the pleading upon him or at any time upon the court's own initiative, the court may order stricken from any pleading any insufficient claim or defense or any redundant, immaterial, impertinent, or scandalous matter.

(G) Consolidation of defenses in motion. A party who makes a motion under this rule may join with it any other motions herein provided for and then available to him. If a party makes a motion under this rule but omits therefrom any defense or objection then available to him which this rule permits to be raised by motion, he shall not thereafter make a motion based on the defense or objection so omitted. He may, however, make such motions as are allowed under subdivision (H)(2) of this rule.

(H) Waiver or preservation of certain defenses.

(1) A defense of lack of jurisdiction over the person, improper venue, insufficiency of process, insufficiency of service of process, or the same action pending in another state court of this state is waived to the extent constitutionally permissible:

(a) if omitted from a motion in the circumstances described in subdivision (G),

(b) if it is neither made by motion under this rule nor included in a responsive pleading or an amendment thereof permitted by Rule 15(A) to be made as a matter of course.

(2) A defense of failure to state a claim upon which relief can be granted, a defense of failure to join an indispensable party under Rule 19(B), and an objection of failure to state a legal defense to a claim may be made in any pleading permitted or ordered under Rule 7(A) or by motion for judgment on the pleadings, or at the trial on the merits.

Rule 13. Counterclaim and cross-claim

(A) Compulsory counterclaims. A pleading shall state as a counterclaim any claim which at the time of serving the pleading the pleader has against any opposing party, if it arises out of the transaction or occurrence that is the subject-matter of the opposing party's claim and does not require for its adjudication the presence of third parties of whom the court cannot acquire jurisdiction. But the pleader need not state the claim if:

(1) at the time the action was commenced the claim was the subject of another pending action; or

(2) the opposing party brought suit upon his claim by attachment or other process by which the court did not acquire jurisdiction to render a personal judgment on that claim, and the pleader is not stating any counterclaim under this rule.

(B) Permissive counterclaims. A pleading may state as a counterclaim any claim against an opposing party not arising out of the transaction or occurrence that is the subject-matter of the opposing party's claim.

(C) Counterclaim exceeding opposing claim. A counterclaim may or may not diminish or defeat the recovery sought by the opposing party. It may claim relief exceeding in amount or different in kind from that sought in the pleading of the opposing party.

(D) Counterclaim against state. This rule shall not be construed to enlarge any right to assert a claim against the state.

(E) Counterclaim maturing or acquired after pleading. A claim which either matured or was acquired by the pleader after serving his pleading may, with the permission of the court, be presented as a counterclaim by supplemental pleading. A counterclaim or cross-claim which is not due may be asserted against a party who is insolvent or the representative of a party who has been subjected to insolvency proceedings, if recovery thereon will be impaired because of such party's insolvency.

(F) Omitted counterclaim. When a pleader fails to set up a counterclaim through oversight, inadvertence, or excusable neglect, or when justice requires, he may by leave of court set up the counterclaim by amendment.

(G) Cross-claim against co-party. A pleading may state as a cross-claim any claim by one party against a co-party.

(H) Joinder of additional parties. Persons other than those made parties to the original action may be made parties to a counterclaim or cross-claim in accordance with the provisions of Rules 14, 19 and 20.

(I) Separate trials--Separate judgments. If the court orders separate trials as provided in Rule 42(B), judgment on a counterclaim or cross-claim may be rendered in accordance with the terms of Rule 54(B) when the court has jurisdiction so to do, even if the claims of the opposing party have been dismissed or otherwise disposed of. In determining whether or not separate trial of a cross-claim shall be ordered, the court shall consider whether the cross-claim:

(1) arises out of the transaction or occurrence or series of transactions or occurrences that is the subject-matter either of the original action or of a counterclaim therein;

(2) relates to any property or contract that is the subject-matter of the original action; or

(3) claims that the person against whom it is asserted is liable to the cross-claimant for all or part of plaintiff's claim against him.

In addition, the court may consider any other relevant factors.

(J) Effect of statute of limitations and other discharges at law. The statute of limitations, a nonclaim statute or other discharge at law shall not bar a claim asserted as a counterclaim to the extent that:

(1) it diminishes or defeats the opposing party's claim if it arises out of the transaction or occurrence that is th subject-matter of the opposing party's claim, or if it could have been asserted as a counterclaim to the opposing party's claim before it (the counterclaim) was barred; or

(2) it or the opposing party's claim relates to payment of or security for the other.

(K) Counterclaim by and against transferees and successors. A counterclaim may be asserted by or against the transferee or successor of a claim subject to the following provisions:

(1) A successor who is a guardian, representative of a decedent's estate, receiver or assignee for the benefit of creditors, trustee or the like may interpose a claim to which he succeeds against claims or proceedings brought in or outside the court of administration. A claim owing by his predecessor may be interposed against any claim brought by such successor in or outside the court of administration without the necessity of filing such claim or cause of action in the administration proceedings.

(2) A transferee or successor of a claim takes it subject to any defense or counterclaim that is the subject-matter of the opposing party's claim; or that is available to the obligor at the time of the assignment or before the obligor received notice of the assignment.

(3) A surety or party with total or partial recourse upon a claim upon which he is being sued may interpose as a counterclaim:

 (a) any claim of his own; and

 (b) any claim owned by the person against whom he has recourse who either has notice of the suit, is a party to the suit, is insolvent, has assigned his claim to the surety or party asserting it, or cannot be found.

 A counterclaim under subdivision (b) must tend to diminish or defeat the opposing party's claim, or it or the opposing claim must relate to payment of or security for the other, unless the person against whom recourse may be had is a party to the suit or the counterclaim has been assigned to the party asserting it; and if recovery on the counterclaim exceeds the opposing party's claim, any excess recovered shall be held in trust for such person against whom there is a right of recourse.

(4) Subsections (1), (2), and (3), above, are subject to subdivision (L) of this rule.

(L) Counterclaim and cross-claim subject to substantive law principles. Counterclaim and cross-claims are subject to restrictions imposed by other statutes and principles of substantive common law and equity, including rules of commercial law, agency, estoppel, contract and the like. In appropriate cases the court may impose terms or conditions upon its judgment or decree and may enter conditional or noncanceling cross judgments to satisfy such restrictions. This provision is intended to deny or limit counterclaims or cross-claims:

(1) where a creditor will receive an unfair priority because a claim is assigned after insolvency proceedings, or assigned before such proceedings if it results in an unlawful preference;

(2) where an unfair priority will be allowed if a surety interposing a claim owned in his own right against the creditor suing on the principal's obligation when the principal is solvent and the creditor is not;

(3) where a claim by or against a representative, such as a guardian, receiver, representative of a decedent's estate, assignee for the benefit of creditors, trustee or the like in his individual capacity is asserted against a claim owing or owed by the estate he represents;

(4) where a claim by or against a partnership or two [2] or more obligors is opposed against or by a claim of an individual to the extent that the individual will be allowed unfairly to profit or if it will adversely affect the rights of creditors; or

(5) where a claim is cut off by a holder in due course or a transferee who is protected under principles of commercial law, estoppel, or contract.

(M) Satisfaction of judgment. Satisfaction of a judgment or credits thereon may be ordered, for sufficient cause, upon notice and motion. "Credits" include any counterclaim which tends to diminish or defeat the judgment, or any counterclaim where it or the opposing claim relates to payment of or security for the other.

Rule 14. Third-party practice

(A) When defendant may bring in third party. A defending party, as a third-party plaintiff, may cause a summons and complaint to be served upon a person not a party to the action who is or may be liable to him for all or part of the plaintiff's claim against him. The third-party plaintiff must file the third-party complaint with his original answer or by leave of court thereafter with good cause shown. The person served with the summons and the third-party complaint, hereinafter called the third-party defendant, as provided in Rules 12 and 13 may make:

(1) his defenses, cross-claims and counterclaims to the third-party plaintiff's claims;

(2) his defenses, counterclaims and cross-claims against any other defendants or third-party defendants;

(3) any defenses or claims which the third-party plaintiff has to the plaintiff's claim which are available to the third-party defendant against the plaintiff; and

(4) any defenses or claims which the third-party defendant has as against the plaintiff.

The plaintiff may assert any claim against the third-party defendant who thereupon may assert his defenses, counterclaims and cross-claims, as provided in Rules 12 and 13. A third-party defendant may proceed under this rule against any person not a party to the action who is or may be liable to him for all or part of the claim made in the action against the third-party defendant.

(B) When plaintiff may bring in third party. When a counterclaim or other claim is asserted against a plaintiff, he may cause a third party to be brought in under circumstances, which, under this rule, would entitle a defendant to do so.

(C) Severance--Parties improperly impleaded. With his responsive pleading or by motion prior thereto, any party may move for severance of a third-party claim or ensuing claim as provided in this rule or for a separate trial thereon. If the third-party defendant is a proper party to the proceedings under any other rule relating to parties, the action shall continue as in other cases where he is made a party.

Rule 15. Amended and supplemental pleadings

(A) Amendments. A party may amend his pleading once as a matter of course at any time before a responsive pleading is served or, if the pleading is one to which no responsive pleading is permitted, and the action has not been placed upon the trial calendar, he may so amend it at any time within thirty [30] days after it is served. Otherwise a party may amend his pleading only by leave of court or by written consent of the adverse party; and leave shall be given when justice so requires. A party shall plead in response to an amended pleading within the time remaining for response to the original pleading or within twenty [20] days after service of the amended pleading, whichever period may be the longer, unless the court otherwise orders.

(B) Amendments to conform to the evidence. When issues not raised by the pleadings are tried by express or implied consent of the parties, they shall be treated in all respects as if they had been raised in the pleadings. Such amendment of the pleadings as may be necessary to cause them to conform to the evidence and to raise these issues may be made upon motion of any party at any time, even after judgment, but failure so to amend does not affect the result of the trial of these issues. If evidence is objected to at the trial on the ground that it is not within the issues made by the pleadings, the court may allow the pleadings to be amended and shall do so freely when the presentation of the merits of the action will be subserved thereby and the objecting party fails to satisfy the court that the admission of such evidence would prejudice him in maintaining his action or defense upon the merits. The court may grant a continuance to enable the objecting party to meet such evidence.

(C) Relation back of amendments. Whenever the claim or defense asserted in the amended pleading arose out of the conduct, transaction, or occurrence set forth or attempted to be set forth in the original pleading, the amendment relates back to the date of the original pleading. An amendment changing the party against whom claim is asserted relates back if the foregoing provision is satisfied and, within one hundred and twenty (120) days of commencement of the action, the party to be brought in by amendment:

(1) has received such notice of the institution of the action that he will not be prejudiced in maintaining his defense on the merits; and

(2) knew or should have known that but for a mistake concerning the identity of the proper party, the action would have been brought against him.

The requirement of subsections (1) and (2) hereof with respect to a governmental organization to be brought into the action as defendant is satisfied:

(1) In the case of a state or governmental organization by delivery or mailing of process to the attorney general or to a governmental executive [Rule 4.6(A)(3)]; or

(2) In the case of a local governmental organization, by delivery or mailing of process to its attorney as provided by statute, to a governmental executive thereof [Rule 4.6(A)(4)], or to the officer holding the office if suit is against the officer or an office.

(D) Supplemental pleadings. Upon motion of a party the court may, upon reasonable notice and upon such terms as are just, permit him to serve a supplemental pleading setting forth transactions or occurrences or events which have happened since the date of the pleading sought to be supplemented. Permission may be granted even though the original pleading is defective in its statement of a claim for relief or defense. If the court deems it advisable that the adverse party plead to the supplemental pleading, it shall so order, specifying the time therefor.

Rule 16. Pre-trial procedure: Formulating issues

(A) When required--Purpose. In any action except criminal cases, the court may in its discretion and shall upon the motion of any party, direct the attorneys for the parties to appear before it for a conference to consider:

(1) the simplification of the issues;

(2) the necessity or desirability of amendments to the pleadings;

(3) the possibility of obtaining admissions of fact and of documents which will avoid unnecessary proof;

(4) a limitation of the number of expert witnesses;

(5) an exchange of names of witnesses to be called during the trial and the general nature of their expected testimony;

(6) the desirability of using one or more types of alternative dispute resolution under the rules therefor;

(7) the desirability of setting deadlines for dispositive motions in light of the date set for trial; and

(8) such other matters as may aid in the disposition of the action.

(B) When called--Notice--Participants. Unless otherwise ordered by the court the pre-trial conference shall not be called until after reasonable opportunity for the completion of discovery.

(1) Notice. The clerks shall give at least thirty [30] days' notice of the pre-trial conference unless otherwise directed by the court.

(2) Participants. At least one [1] attorney planning to take part in the trial shall appear for each of the parties and participate in the pre-trial conference.

(C) Conference of attorneys. Unless otherwise ordered by the court, at least ten [10] days prior to the pre-trial conference, attorneys for each of the parties shall meet and confer for the following purposes:

(1) Exhibits. Each attorney shall mark for identification and provide opposing counsel an opportunity to inspect and copy all exhibits which he expects to introduce at the trial. Numbers or marks placed on such exhibits shall be prefixed with the symbol "P/T", denoting its pre-trial designation. When the exhibit is introduced at the trial of the case, the "P/T" designation will be stricken and the exhibits must also indicate the party identifying same.

Exhibits of the character which prohibit or make impracticable their production at conference shall be identified and notice given of their intended use. Necessary arrangements must be made to afford opposing counsel an opportunity to examine such exhibits.

(2) Exhibit stipulations. Written stipulations shall be prepared with reference to all exhibits exchanged or identified. The stipulations shall contain all agreements of the parties with reference to the exchanged and identified exhibits, and shall include, but not be limited to, the agreement of the parties with reference to the authenticity of the exhibits, their admissibility in evidence, their use in opening statements, and the provisions made for the inspection of identified exhibits. The original of the exhibit stipulations shall be presented to the court at the pre-trial conference.

(3) Fact stipulation. The attorneys shall stipulate in writing with reference to all facts and issues not in genuine dispute. The original of the stipulations shall be presented to the court at the time of the pre-trial conference.

(4) Exchange list of witnesses. Attorneys for each of the parties shall furnish opposing counsel with the written list of the names and addresses of all witnesses then known. The original of each witness list shall be presented to the court at the time of the pre-trial conference.

(5) Discuss Administrative Rule 9(G) issues that may arise during the proceedings.

(6) Discuss settlement. The possibility of compromise settlement shall be fully discussed and explored.

(D) Preparation for conference of attorneys and pre-trial. Each attorney shall completely familiarize himself with all aspects of the case in advance of the conference of attorneys and be prepared to enter into stipulations with reference to as many facts and issues and exhibits as possible.

(E) Duty to arrange conference. It shall be the duty of counsel for both plaintiff and defendant to arrange for the conference of attorneys at least ten [10] days in advance of the pre-trial conference.

(F) Refusal to stipulate. If, following the conference of attorneys, either party determines that there are other facts or exhibits that should be stipulated and which opposing counsel refuses to stipulate upon, he shall compile a list of such facts or exhibits and furnish same to opposing counsel at least two [2] days in advance of the pre-trial conference. The original of the list shall be presented to the court at the time of the pre-trial conference.

(G) Witnesses or exhibits discovered subsequent to conference of attorneys and before a pre-trial conference. If, after the conference of the attorneys and before the pre-trial conference, counsel discovers additional exhibits or names of additional witnesses, the same information required to be disclosed at the conference of the attorneys shall be immediately furnished opposing counsel. The original of any such disclosures shall be presented to the court at the time of the pre-trial conference.

(H) More than one pre-trial conference. If necessary or advisable, the court may adjourn the pre-trial conference from time to time or may order an additional pre-trial conference.

(I) Witnesses or exhibits discovered subsequent to pre-trial conference. If, following the pre-trial conference or during trial, counsel discovers additional exhibits or the names of additional witnesses, the same information required to be disclosed at the conference between attorneys shall be immediately furnished opposing counsel. The original of any such disclosure shall immediately be filed with the court and shall indicate the date it was furnished opposing counsel.

(J) Pre-trial order. The court shall make an order which recites the action taken at the conference, the amendments allowed to the pleading, and the agreements made by the parties as to any of the matters considered which limit the issues for trial to those not disposed of by admissions or agreement of counsel, and such order when entered shall control the subsequent course of action, unless modified thereafter to prevent manifest injustice. The court in its discretion may establish by rule a pre-trial calendar on which actions may be placed for consideration as above provided, and may either confine the calendar to jury actions or non-jury actions or extend it to all actions.

(K) Sanctions: Failure to appear. If without just excuse or because of failure to give reasonable attention to the matter, no appearance is made on behalf of a party at a pre-trial conference, or if an attorney is grossly unprepared to participate in the conference, the court may order either one or both of the following:

(1) the payment by the delinquent attorney or party of the reasonable expenses, including attorney's fees, to the aggrieved party; or

(2) take such other action as may be appropriate.

Rule 17. Parties plaintiff and defendant--Capacity

(A) Real party in interest. Every action shall be prosecuted in the name of the real party in interest.

(1) An executor, administrator, guardian, bailee, trustee of an express trust, a party with whom or in whose name a contract has been made for the benefit of another, or a party authorized by statute may sue in his

own name without joining with him the party for whose benefit the action is brought, but stating his relationship and the capacity in which he sues.

(2) When a statute provides for an action by this state on the relation of another, the action may be brought in the name of the person for whose use or benefit the statute was intended.

No action shall be dismissed on the ground that it is not prosecuted in the name of the real party in interest until a reasonable time after objection has been allowed for the real party in interest to ratify the action, or to be joined or substituted in the action. Such ratification, joinder, or substitution shall have the same effect as if the action had been commenced initially in the name of the real party in interest.

(B) Capacity to sue or be sued. The capacity of a party to sue or be sued shall be determined by the law of this state, including its conflicts rules, except that a partnership or unincorporated association may sue or be sued in its common name.

(C) Infants or incompetent persons--Unborn, unknown, and unlocated persons. An infant or incompetent person may sue or be sued in any action:

(1) in his own name;

(2) in his own name by a guardian ad litem or a next friend;

(3) in the name of his representative, if the representative is a court-appointed general guardian, committee, conservator, guardian of the estate or other like fiduciary.

The court, upon its own motion or upon the motion of any party, must notify and allow the representative named in subsection (3) of this subdivision, if he is known, to represent an infant or incompetent person, and be joined as an additional party in his representative capacity. If an infant or incompetent person is not represented, or is not adequately represented, the court shall appoint a guardian ad litem for him. The court may, in its discretion, appoint a guardian ad litem or an attorney for persons who are institutionalized, who are not yet born or in being, who are unknown, who are known but cannot be located, or who are in such position that they cannot procure reasonable representation. The court shall make such other orders as it deems proper for the protection of such parties or persons. Persons with claims against the estate of the ward or against the guardian of his estate as such may proceed under this rule or provisions applicable to guardianship proceedings. It shall not be necessary that the person for whom guardianship is sought shall be represented by a guardian ad litem in such proceedings. Nothing herein shall affect the right of a guardian to sue or be sued in his personal capacity.

The court, in its discretion, may honor the infant's or incompetent's choice of next friend or guardian ad litem, but the court may deny approval or remove a person who is not qualified. A next friend or guardian under subsection (C) of this rule may be required by the court to furnish bond or additional bond and shall be subject to the rules applicable to guardians of the estate with respect to duties, terms of the bond required, accounting, compensation and termination.

(D) Sex, marital and parental status. For the purposes of suing or being sued there shall be no distinction between men and women or between men and women because of marital or parental status; provided, however, that this subdivision (D) shall not apply to actions in tort.

(E) Partnerships and unincorporated associations. A partnership or an unincorporated association may sue or be sued in its common name. A judgment by or against the partnership or unincorporated association shall bind the organization as if it were an entity. A money judgment against the partnership or unincorporated association shall not bind an individual partner or member unless he is named as a party or is bound as a member of a class in an appropriate action (Rules 23 and 23.2).

(F) Unknown persons. When the name or existence of a person is unknown, he may be named as an unknown party, and when his true name is discovered his name may be inserted by amendment at any time.

Rule 17.1. Parties: State as party--Attorney general

If in any action or proceeding involving real property, instituted in any court of this state, it appears from the allegations of any pleading filed therein that the state of Indiana has, or claims to have a lien upon or an interest in such real estate, the state may be made a party defendant to the action, and shall be bound by any judgment or decree rendered thereon. Service of summons shall be made upon the Attorney General as provided in Rule 4.8. It shall be the duty of the Attorney General, in person or by deputy to appear and defend such proceedings or suit, on behalf of the state of Indiana. The Attorney General may, in his discretion, designate the prosecuting attorney of the circuit in which such action is pending as his deputy for the purpose of defending such proceedings or suit on behalf of the state of Indiana. After the prosecuting attorney enters his appearance as such deputy, pleadings under Rule 5 shall be served upon him for and on behalf of the Attorney General. The state may appeal from such judgment or decree, in like manner and under the same terms and conditions as other parties in like cases.

his rule is meant, without limitation, to apply to actions to foreclose a mortgage or other lien on real estate, to subject any eal estate to sale, or to partition or quiet title to real estate.

urther, in any case in which the Attorney General represents the State of Indiana, the judge presiding in the case where uch cause is pending, shall promptly notify the Attorney General by United States mail, addressed to his office in ndianapolis, Indiana, of any ruling made in such cause or of the fixing of a date for the trial thereof.

Rule 18. Joinder of claims and remedies

(A) Joinder of claims. A party asserting a claim for relief as an original claim, counterclaim, cross-claim, or third-party claim, may join, either as independent or as alternate claims, as many claims, whether legal, equitable, or statutory as he has against an opposing party.

(B) Joinder of remedies--Fraudulent conveyances. Whenever a claim is one heretofore cognizable only after another claim has been prosecuted to a conclusion, the two [2] claims may be joined in a single action; but the court shall grant relief in that action only in accordance with the relative substantive rights of the parties. In particular, a plaintiff may state a claim for money and a claim to have set aside a conveyance fraudulent as to him, without first having obtained a judgment establishing the claim for money.

Rule 19. Joinder of person needed for just adjudication

(A) Persons to be joined if feasible. A person who is subject to service of process shall be joined as a party in the action if:

(1) in his absence complete relief cannot be accorded among those already parties; or

(2) he claims an interest relating to the subject of the action and is so situated that the disposition of the action in his absence may:

(a) as a practical matter impair or impede his ability to protect that interest, or

(b) leave any of the persons already parties subject to a substantial risk of incurring double, multiple, or otherwise inconsistent obligations by reason of his claimed interest.

If he has not been so joined, the court shall order that he be made a party. If he should join as a plaintiff but refuses to do so, he may be made a defendant.

(B) Determination by court whenever joinder not feasible. Notwithstanding subdivision (A) of this rule when a person described in subsection (1) or (2) thereof is not made a party, the court may treat the absent party as not indispensable and allow the action to proceed without him; or the court may treat such absent party as indispensable and dismiss the action if he is not subject to process. In determining whether or not a party is indispensable the court in its discretion and in equity and good conscience shall consider the following factors:

(1) the extent to which a judgment rendered in the person's absence might be prejudicial to him or those already parties;

(2) the extent to which, by protective provisions in the judgment, by the shaping of relief, or other measures, the prejudice can be lessened or avoided;

(3) whether a judgment rendered in the person's absence will be adequate;

(4) whether the plaintiff will have an adequate remedy if the action is dismissed for nonjoinder.

(C) Pleading nonjoinder. Nonjoinder under this rule may be raised by motion as provided in Rule 12(B)(7).

(D) Exception of class actions. This rule is subject to the provisions of Rule 23.

(E) Parties not indispensable--Joinder of obligors, assignors, and subrogees and subrogors.

(1) Joint obligors. Joinder of all the parties to a joint and several obligation and to a joint obligation, including a partnership obligation, shall not be required, and joint or separate action may be brought against one or more of such obligors who shall be subject to permissive joinder as provided in Rule 20. A judgment against fewer than all does not merge or bar the claim against those not made parties for that reason.

(2) Assignor of claim. Joinder of the assignor or transferor of a claim or chose in action shall not be required in a suit by the assignee who establishes his title by appropriate pleading and proof, but such assignor or transferor shall be subject to permissive joinder as provided in Rule 20.

(3) Subrogation.

(a) A subrogor may enforce the claim to the extent of his interest or in full without joining the subrogee.

(b) The subrogee may enforce the claim to the extent that he establishes his title or interest by appropriate pleading and proof without joining the subrogor.

(c) In such cases the subrogor or subrogee shall be subject to permissive joinder as provided in Rule 20.

Any recovery by the subrogor to the extent that such recovery is owned by a subrogee shall be made as representative and trustee for the subrogee.

(F) Governmental organizations and representatives thereof as parties. Suits by or against a governmental organization or governmental representative relating to the acts, power or authority of such organization or representative, including acts under purported power or authority or color thereof by such organization or representative, shall be governed by this provision.

(1) Suits by or against a governmental organization or against a representative in his official capacity shall be brought in the name of the governmental organization. Suits naming a governmental representative by his official title or by his name along with his official title shall be deemed to name and include the governmental organization which he represents, and suits naming an unofficial branch, office or unit of a governmental organization shall be deemed to name and include the governmental organization of which it is a part; but the court upon its own motion or the motion of any party may require the omitted and proper governmental organization to be included at any time.

(2) Other government organizations and governmental representatives of the same or other governmental organizations may be joined or made parties to suits in which a governmental organization is named as a party in accordance with the provisions of these rules relating to parties. Failure to name, or improper naming of a governmental organization or a governmental representative shall be subject to the provisions of these rules relating to parties.

(3) A judgment for or against a governmental organization shall also bind affected or successive representatives of such organization. When a governmental representative is named as a party in his individual name or in his individual name along with his official title, the judgment, in an appropriate case may bind him in his individual capacity, but no judgment against him in his individual capacity shall be rendered against him unless he is so named. No action against a governmental organization or against a governmental representative in his official capacity shall be abated, affected or delayed because of the death, incapacity or replacement of a named or unnamed governmental representative, or because of the fact that the name, functions or existence of the governmental organization have been altered or terminated. In either case the action shall proceed without substitution of successors who shall be bound by the judgment in their official capacity.

Rule 20. Permissive joinder of parties

(A) Permissive joinder.

(1) All persons may join in one [1] action as plaintiffs if they assert any right to relief jointly, severally, or in the alternative in respect of or arising out of the same transaction, occurrence, or series of transactions or occurrences and if any question of law or fact common to all these persons will arise in the action.

(2) All persons may be joined in one [1] action as defendants if there is asserted against them jointly, severally, or in the alternative, any right to relief in respect of, or arising out of, the same transaction, occurrence, or series of transactions or occurrences and if any question of law or fact common to all defendants will arise in the action.

A plaintiff or defendant need not be interested in obtaining or defending against all the relief demanded. Judgment may be given for one or more of the plaintiffs according to their respective rights to relief, and against one or more defendants according to their respective liabilities. Unwilling plaintiffs who could join under this rule may be joined by a plaintiff as defendants, and the defendant may make any persons who could be joined under this rule parties by alleging their interest therein with a prayer that their rights in the controversy be determined, along with any counterclaim or cross-claim against them, if any, as if they had been originally joined as parties.

(B) Separate trials. The court may make such orders as will prevent a party from being embarrassed, delayed, or put to expense by the inclusion of a party against whom he asserts no claim and who asserts no claim against him, and may order separate trials of the entire case or separate issues therein, or make other orders to prevent delay or prejudice.

Rule 21. Misjoinder and non-joinder of parties; venue and jurisdiction over the subject-matter

(A) Effect of misjoinder and non-joinder. Misjoinder of parties is not ground for dismissal of an action. Except as otherwise provided in these rules, failure to name another person as a party or include him in the action is not ground for dismissal; but such omission is subject to the right of such person to intervene or of an opposing party to name or include him in the action as permitted by these rules. Subject to its sound discretion and on motion of any party or of its own initiative, the court may order parties dropped or added at any stage of the action and on such terms as are just and will avoid delay. Any claim against a party may be severed and proceeded with separately. Incorrect names and misnomers may be corrected by amendment under Rule 15 at any time.

(B) Effect of venue or jurisdiction over part of case. The court shall have venue and authority over all persons or claims required to be joined or permissively joined, impleaded or included by intervention, interpleader, counterclaim or cross-claim if it has venue or is authorized to determine any claim asserted between any of the parties thereto, notwithstanding any requirement of venue or of jurisdiction over the subject-matter applicable to other claims or other parties. The court may transfer the proceedings to the proper court if it determines that venue or authority of the court is dependent upon a claim, or a claim by or against a particular party which appears from the pleadings, or proves to be a sham or made in bad faith; and if another action is pending in this state by or against a person upon the same claim at the time he becomes a party, the court may dismiss the action as to him, or in its sound discretion, it may order all or part of the proceedings to be consolidated with the first pending action.

Rule 22. Interpleader

(A) Plaintiff or defendant. Persons having claims against the plaintiff may be joined as defendants and required to interplead when their claims are such that the plaintiff is or may be exposed to double or multiple liability. It is not ground for objection to the joinder that the claims of the several claimants or the titles on which their claims depend do not have a common origin or are not identical but are adverse to and independent of one another, or that the plaintiff avers that he is not liable in whole or part to any or all of the claimants. A defendant exposed to similar liability may obtain such interpleader by way of cross-claim or counterclaim. The provisions of this rule supplement and do not in any way limit the joinder of parties permitted in Rule 20.

(B) Extension of statutory interpleader. This rule shall extend, but not diminish or reduce the right to interpleader provided by statute.

(C) Sufficiency of complaint or answer seeking interpleader. A complaint or answer seeking interpleader under Rule 22(A) is sufficient if:

(1) it admits that a liability is owing or it states that a totally or partially unfounded liability is asserted to be owing to either one or more of the parties interpleaded;

(2) it declares that because of such claims the person seeking interpleader is or may be exposed to double or multiple liability; and

(3) it prays that the parties interpleaded assert their claims against the party seeking interpleader and against each other.

The complaint may also show, if such is the fact, that the person seeking interpleader has deposited with the court money, or property, or a bond securing performance. It also may include appropriate prayers for equitable relief, including injunction against other nonpending suits by the parties interpleaded, against the person seeking interpleader or among themselves. Except to the extent that the issues are raised by the pleadings of the person seeking interpleader, the claims of those interpleaded, whether dependent or independent, may be pleaded in the same manner as if the claims were counterclaims or cross-claims under Rule 13 and within the time as prescribed by Rule 6. Incorrectness of the interpleader under Rule 22(A) is grounds for dismissal as provided in Rule 12(B)(6). New service against defaulting parties required by Rule 5(A) shall not apply to the responsive pleadings filed by parties named to interpleader proceedings under Rule 22(A) unless ordered by the court. Trial of the issues may be held at one [1] hearing or in successive stages at the sound discretion of the court and subject to Rule 42.

(D) Release from liability--Deposit or delivery. Any party seeking interpleader, as provided in subdivision (A) of this rule, may deposit with the court the amount claimed, or deliver to the court or as otherwise directed by the court the property claimed, and the court may thereupon order such party discharged from liability as to such claims, and the action continued as between the claimants of such money or property.

Rule 23. Class actions

(A) Prerequisites to a class action. One or more members of a class may sue or be sued as representative parties on behalf of all only if:

(1) the class is so numerous that joinder of all members is impracticable;

(2) there are questions of law or fact common to the class;

(3) the claims or defenses of the representative parties are typical of the claims or defenses of the class; and

(4) the representative parties will fairly and adequately protect the interests of the class.

(B) Class actions maintainable. An action may be maintained as a class action if the prerequisites of subdivision (A) are satisfied, and in addition:

(1) the prosecution of separate actions by or against individual members of the class would create a risk of:

(a) inconsistent or varying adjudications with respect to individual members of the class which would establish incompatible standards of conduct for the party opposing the class, or

(b) adjudications with respect to individual members of the class which would as a practical matter be dispositive of the interest of the other members not parties to the adjudications or substantially impair or impede their ability to protect their interests; or

(2) the party opposing the class has acted or refused to act on grounds generally applicable to the class, thereby making appropriate final injunctive relief or corresponding declaratory relief with respect to the class as a whole; or

(3) the court finds that the questions of law or fact common to the members of the class predominate over any questions affecting only individual members, and that a class action is superior to other available methods for the fair and efficient adjudication of the controversy. The matters pertinent to the findings include:

(a) the interest of members of the class in individually controlling the prosecution or defense of separate actions;

(b) the extent and nature of any litigation concerning the controversy already commenced by or against members of the class;

(c) the desirability or undesirability of concentrating the litigation of the claims in the particular forum;

(d) the difficulties likely to be encountered in the management of a class action.

(C) Determination by order whether class action to be maintained--Notice--Judgment--Actions conducted partially as class actions.

(1) As soon as practicable after the commencement of an action brought as a class action, the court, upon hearing or waiver of hearing, shall determine by order whether it is to be so maintained. An order under this subdivision may be conditional, and may be altered or amended before the decision on the merits.

(2) In any class action maintained under subdivision (B)(3), the court shall direct to the members of the class the best notice practicable under the circumstances, including individual notice to all members who can be identified through reasonable effort. The notice shall advise each member that:

(a) the court will exclude him from the class if he so requests by a specified date;

(b) the judgment, whether favorable or not, will include all members who do not request exclusion; and

(c) any member who does not request exclusion may, if he desires, enter an appearance through his counsel.

(3) The judgment in an action maintained as a class action under subdivision (B)(1) or (B)(2), whether or not favorable to the class, shall include and describe those whom the court finds to be members of the class. The judgment in an action maintained as a class action under subdivision (B)(3), whether or not favorable to the class, shall include and specify or describe those to whom the notice provided in subdivision (C)(2) was directed, and who have not requested exclusion, and whom the court finds to be members of the class.

(4) When appropriate:

(a) an action may be brought or maintained as a class action with respect to particular issues; or

(b) a class may be divided into subclasses and each subclass treated as a class, and the provisions of this rule shall then be construed and applied accordingly.

(D) Orders in conduct of actions. In the conduct of actions to which this rule applies, the court may make appropriate orders:

(1) determining the course of proceedings or prescribing measures to prevent undue repetition or complication in the presentation of evidence or argument;

(2) requiring, for the protection of the members of the class or otherwise for the fair conduct of the action, that notice be given in such manner as the court may direct to some or all of the members of any step in the action, or of the proposed extent of the judgment, or of the opportunity of members to signify whether they

consider the representation fair and adequate, to intervene and present claims or defenses, or otherwise to come into the action;

(3) imposing conditions on the representative parties or on intervenors;

(4) requiring that the pleadings be amended to eliminate therefrom allegations as to representation of absent persons, and that the action proceed accordingly;

(5) dealing with similar procedural matters.

The orders may be combined with an order under Rule 16, and may be altered or amended as may be desirable from time to time. The court shall allow reasonable attorney's fees and reasonable expenses incurred from a fund recovered for the benefit of a class under this section and the court may apportion such recovery among different attorneys.

(E) Dismissal or compromise. A class action shall not be dismissed or compromised without the approval of the court, and notice of the proposed dismissal or compromise shall be given to all members of the class in such manner as the court directs.

(F) Disposition of Residual Funds.

(1) "Residual Funds" are funds that remain after the payment of all approved class member claims, expenses, litigation costs, attorneys' fees, and other court-approved disbursements to implement the relief granted. Nothing in this rule is intended to limit the trial court from approving a settlement that does not create residual funds.

(2) Any order entering a judgment or approving a proposed compromise of a class action certified under this rule that establishes a process for identifying and compensating members of the class shall provide for the disbursement of residual funds, unless otherwise agreed. In matters where the claims process has been exhausted and residual funds remain, not less than twenty-five percent (25%) of the residual funds shall be disbursed to the Indiana Bar Foundation to support the activities and programs of the Coalition for Court Access and its *pro bono* districts. The court may disburse the balance of any residual funds beyond the minimum percentage to the Indiana Bar Foundation or to any other entity for purposes that have a direct or indirect relationship to the objectives of the underlying litigation or otherwise promote the substantive or procedural interests of members of the certified class.

Rule 23.1. Derivative actions by shareholders

In a derivative action brought by one or more shareholders or members or holders of an interest in such shares or membership, legal or equitable, to enforce a right of a corporation or of an unincorporated association, the corporation or association having failed to enforce a right which may properly be asserted by it, the complaint shall be verified and shall allege that the plaintiff was a shareholder or member or holder of an interest, legal or equitable, in such shares or membership at the time of the transaction or any part thereof of which he complains or that his share or membership thereafter devolved on him by operation of law, and the complaint shall also allege with particularity the efforts, if any, made by the plaintiff, to obtain the action he desires from the directors or comparable authority and the reasons for his failure to obtain the action or for not making the effort. The derivative action may not be maintained if it appears that the plaintiff does not fairly and adequately represent the interests of the shareholders or members similarly situated in enforcing the right of the corporation or association. The action shall not be dismissed or compromised without the approval of the court, and notice of the proposed dismissal or compromise shall be given to shareholders or members in such manner as the court directs.

Rule 23.2. Actions relating to unincorporated associations

In addition to an action brought by or against an unincorporated association under Rule 17(E), an action may be brought against the members of an unincorporated association as a class by naming certain members as representative parties if it appears that the members bringing suit or served with process or the representative parties will fairly and adequately protect the interests of the association and its members. In the conduct of the action the court may make appropriate orders corresponding with those described in Rule 23(D), and the procedure for dismissal or compromise of the action shall correspond with that provided in Rule 23(E).

Rule 24. Intervention

(A) Intervention of right. Upon timely motion anyone shall be permitted to intervene in an action:

(1) when a statute confers an unconditional right to intervene; or

(2) when the applicant claims an interest relating to a property, fund or transaction which is the subject of the action and he is so situated that the disposition of the action may as a practical matter impair or impede his

ability to protect his interest in the property, fund or transaction, unless the applicant's interest is adequately represented by existing parties.

(B) Permissive intervention. Upon timely filing of his motion anyone may be permitted to intervene in an action:

(1) when a statute confers a conditional right to intervene; or

(2) when an applicant's claim or defense and the main action have a question of law or fact in common. When a party to an action relies for ground of claim or defense upon any statute or executive order administered by a federal or state governmental officer or agency or upon any regulation, order, requirement, or agreement issued or made pursuant to the statute or executive administrative order, the governmental unit upon timely application may be permitted to intervene in the action. In exercising its discretion the court shall consider whether the intervention will unduly delay or prejudice the adjudication of the rights of the original parties.

(C) Procedure. A person desiring to intervene shall serve a motion to intervene upon the parties as provided in Rule 5. The motion shall state the grounds therefor and set forth or include by reference the claim, defense or matter for which intervention is sought. Intervention after trial or after judgment for purposes of a motion under Rules 50, 59, or 60, or an appeal may be allowed upon motion. The court's determination upon a motion to intervene shall be interlocutory for all purposes unless made final under Trial Rule 54(B).

Rule 25. Substitution of parties

(A) Death.

(1) If a party dies and the claim is not thereby extinguished, the court may order substitution of the proper parties. The motion for substitution may be made by the court, any party or by the successors or representatives of the deceased party and, together with the notice of hearing, shall be served on the parties as provided in Rule 5 and upon persons not parties in the manner provided in Rule 4 for the service of summons. Motion for substitution may be made before or after judgment, and if substitution is not reflected in the papers upon which the appeal is based, any party shall, by notice filed with the Clerk of the court on appeal, advise the court on appeal of the substitution of any party. However, if the case is returned to a lower court after the judgment or order upon appeal becomes final, the motion may then be made in such lower court.

(2) In the event of the death of one or more of the plaintiffs or of one or more of the defendants in an action in which the right sought to be enforced survives only to the surviving plaintiffs or only against the surviving defendants, the action does not abate. The death may be suggested upon the record and the action shall proceed in favor of or against the surviving parties.

(B) Incompetency. If a party becomes incompetent, the court upon motion served as provided in subdivision (A) of this rule may allow the action to be continued by or against his representative in the same manner as against a decedent party.

(C) Transfer of interest. In case of any transfer of interest, the action may be continued by or against the original party, unless the court upon motion directs the person to whom the interest is transferred to be substituted in the action or joined with the original party. Service of the motion shall be made as provided in subdivision (A) of this rule.

(D) Persons substituted on death--Personal representative or successors in interest. The proper party or parties to be substituted for the party who dies under subsection (1) of subdivision (A) of this rule includes:

(1) a successor in interest whose rights or obligations do not pass to the representative of the deceased party's estate; or

(2) if the interest passes to or binds the representative of the deceased party's estate, either such representative or, if it is established that the estate of the deceased party is closed or that opening of such estate is unnecessary, the successor of such estate.

(E) Necessity of filing claims against estate when representative substituted--Proceedings to enforce judgment, execution and judgment liens. A claim based upon a judgment against a party who dies before or after judgment is entered shall be allowed by the court administering his estate even though the claim is not filed with such court if the representative of such estate is substituted as a party within the time when such claim or judgment could have been filed as a claim against the estate under the probate code. Judgments upon an action against a party who dies, whether entered before or after his death shall be satisfied from the assets of his estate by the decedent's representative, and no execution, proceedings supplemental or enforcement orders shall issue on the judgment after the party has died as against his property; but this provision shall not prevent enforcement of execution liens, judgment liens, liens acquired by judicial proceedings, security interests, mortgages, liens or interests in property acquired before his death and being enforced by or under the judgment, subject to any rights of the representative to redeem or stay enforcement as now provided by law.

(F) Public Officers; Death or Separation from Office.

(1) When a public officer is a party to an action or other proceeding in an official capacity and during its pendency dies, resigns, or otherwise ceases to hold office, the action does not abate and the officer's successor is automatically substituted as a party. Proceedings following substitution shall be in the name of the substituted party, but any misnomer not affecting the substantial rights of the parties shall be disregarded. An order of substitution may be entered at any time, but the omission to enter such an order shall not affect the substitution.

(2) A public officer who sues or is sued in an official capacity may be described as a party by the officer's official title rather than by name; but the court may require the officer's name to be added.

Rule 26. General provisions governing discovery

(A) Discovery methods. Parties may obtain discovery by one or more of the following methods:

(1) depositions upon oral examination or written questions;

(2) written interrogatories;

(3) production of documents, electronically stored information, or things or permission to enter upon land or other property, for inspection and other purposes;

(4) physical and mental examination;

(5) requests for admission.

Unless the court orders otherwise under subdivision (C) of this rule, the frequency of use of these methods is not limited.

(A.1) Electronic Format. In addition to service under Rule 5(B) or a .pdf format electronic copy, a party propounding or responding to interrogatories, requests for production or requests for admission shall comply with (a) or (b) of this subsection.

(a) The party shall serve the discovery request or response in an electronic format (either on a disk or as an electronic document attachment) in any commercially available word processing software system. If transmitted on disk, each disk shall be labeled, identifying the caption of the case, the document, and the word processing version in which it is being submitted. If more than one disk is used for the same document, each disk shall be labeled and also shall be sequentially numbered. If transmitted by electronic mail, the document must be accompanied by electronic memorandum providing the forgoing identifying information.

or

(b) The party shall serve the opposing party with a verified statement that the attorney or party appearing pro se lacks the equipment and is unable to transmit the discovery as required by this rule.

(B) Scope of discovery. Unless otherwise limited by order of the court in accordance with these rules, the scope of discovery is as follows:

(1) In general. Parties may obtain discovery regarding any matter, not privileged, which is relevant to the subject-matter involved in the pending action, whether it relates to the claim or defense of the party seeking discovery or the claim or defense of any other party, including the existence, description, nature, custody, condition and location of any books, documents, or other tangible things and the identity and location of persons having knowledge of any discoverable matter. It is not ground for objection that the information sought will be inadmissible at the trial if the information sought appears reasonably calculated to lead to the discovery of admissible evidence.

The frequency or extent of use of the discovery methods otherwise permitted under these rules and by any local rule shall be limited by the court if it determines that: (i) the discovery sought is unreasonably cumulative or duplicative, or is obtainable from some other source that is more convenient, less burdensome, or less expensive; (ii) the party seeking discovery has had ample opportunity by discovery in the action to obtain the information sought or; (iii) the burden or expense of the proposed discovery outweighs its likely benefit, taking into account the needs of the case, the amount in controversy, the parties' resources, the importance of the issues at stake in the litigation, and the importance of the proposed discovery in resolving the issues. The court may act upon its own initiative after reasonable notice or pursuant to a motion under Rule 26(C).

(2) Insurance agreements. A party may obtain discovery of the existence and contents of any insurance agreement under which any person carrying on an insurance business may be liable to satisfy part or all of a judgment which may be entered in the action or to indemnify or reimburse for payments made to satisfy the judgment. Information concerning the insurance agreement is not by reason of disclosure admissible i evidence at trial. For purposes of this paragraph, an application for insurance shall not be treated as part c an insurance agreement.

(3) Trial preparation: Materials. Subject to the provisions of subdivision (B)(4) of this rule, a party may obtair discovery of documents and tangible things otherwise discoverable under subdivision (B)(1) of this rule and prepared in anticipation of litigation or for trial by or for another party or by or for that other party's representative (including his attorney, consultant, surety, indemnitor, insurer, or agent) only upon a showing that the party seeking discovery has substantial need of the materials in the preparation of his cas and that he is unable without undue hardship to obtain the substantial equivalent of the materials by othe means. In ordering discovery of such materials when the required showing has been made, the court shall protect against disclosure of the mental impressions, conclusions, opinions, or legal theories of an attorne or other representative of a party concerning the litigation.

A party may obtain without the required showing a statement concerning the action or its subject matter previously made by that party. Upon request, a person not a party may obtain without the required showing a statement concerning the action or its subject matter previously made by that person. If the request is refused, the person may move for a court order. The provisions of Rule 37(A)(4) apply to the award of expenses incurred in relation to the motion. For purposes of this paragraph, a statement previously made is

(a) a written statement signed or otherwise adopted approved by the person making it, or

(b) a stenographic, mechanical, electrical, or other recording, or a transcription thereof, which is a substantially verbatim recital of an oral statement by the person making it and contemporaneously recorded.

(4) Trial Preparation: Experts. Discovery of facts known and opinions held by experts, otherwise discoverable under the provisions of subdivision (B)(1) of this rule and acquired or developed in anticipation of litigation or for trial, may be obtained as follows:

(a) (i) A party may through interrogatories require any other party to identify each person whom the other party expects to call as an expert witness at trial, to state the subject matter on which the expert is expected to testify, and to state the substance of the facts and opinions to which the expert is expected to testify and a summary of the grounds for each opinion.

(ii) Upon motion, the court may order further discovery by other means, subject to such restrictions as to scope and such provisions, pursuant to subdivision (B)(4)(c) of this rule, concerning fees and expenses as the court may deem appropriate.

(b) A party may discover facts known or opinions held by an expert who has been retained or specially employed by another party in anticipation of litigation or preparation for trial and who is not expected to be called as a witness at trial, only as provided in Rule 35(B) or upon a showing of exceptional circumstances under which it is impracticable for the party seeking discovery to obtain facts or opinions on the same subject by other means,

(c) Unless manifest injustice would result,

(i) the court shall require that the party seeking discovery pay the expert a reasonable fee for time spent in responding to discovery under subdivision (B)(4)(a)(ii) and (B)(4)(b) of this rule; and

(ii) with respect to discovery obtained under subdivision (B)(4)(a)(ii) of this rule the court may require, and with respect to discovery obtained under subdivision (B)(4)(b) of this rule the court shall require, the party seeking discovery to pay the other party a fair portion of the fees and expenses reasonably incurred by the latter party in obtaining facts and opinions from the expert.

(5) Claims of Privilege or Protection.

(a) Information withheld. When a party withholds information otherwise discoverable under these rules by claiming that it is privileged or subject to protection as trial preparation material, the party shall make the claim expressly and shall describe the nature of the documents, communications, or things not produced or disclosed in a manner that, without revealing information itself privileged or protected, will enable other parties to assess the applicability of the privilege or protection.

(b) Information produced. If information is produced in discovery that is subject to a claim of privilege or protection as trial-preparation material, the party making the claim may notify any party that received the information of the claim and the basis for it. After being notified, a party must promptly return, sequester, or destroy the specified information and any copies it has and may not use or disclose the information until the claim is resolved. A receiving party may promptly present the information to the court under seal for a determination of the claim. If the receiving party disclosed the information before being notified, it must take reasonable steps to retrieve it. The producing party must preserve the information until the claim is resolved.

(C) Protective orders. Upon motion by any party or by the person from whom discovery is sought, and for good cause shown, the court in which the action is pending or alternatively, on matters relating to a deposition, the court in the county where the deposition is being taken, may make any order which justice requires to protect a party or person from annoyance, embarrassment, oppression, or undue burden or expense, including one or more of the following:

(1) that the discovery not be had;

(2) that the discovery may be had only on specified terms and conditions, including a designation of the time or place;

(3) that the discovery may be had only by a method of discovery other than that selected by the party seeking discovery;

(4) that certain matters not be inquired into, or that the scope of the discovery be limited to certain matters;

(5) that discovery be conducted with no one present except the parties and their attorneys and persons designated by the court;

(6) that a deposition after being sealed be opened only by order of the court;

(7) that a trade secret or other confidential research, development, or commercial information not be disclosed or be disclosed only in a designated way;

(8) that the parties simultaneously file specified documents or information enclosed in sealed envelopes to be opened as directed by the court. If the motion for a protective order is denied in whole or in part, the court may, on such terms and conditions as are just, order that any party or person provide or permit discovery. The provisions of Trial Rule 37(A)(4) apply to the award of expenses incurred in relation to the motion.

(9) that a party need not provide discovery of electronically stored information from sources that the party identifies as not reasonably accessible because of undue burden or cost. On motion to compel discovery or for a protective order, the party from whom discovery is sought must show that the information is not reasonably accessible because of undue burden or cost. If that showing is made, the court may nonetheless order discovery from such sources if the requesting party shows good cause. The court may specify conditions for the discovery.

(D) Sequence and timing of discovery. Unless the court upon motion, for the convenience of parties and witnesses and in the interests of justice, orders otherwise, methods of discovery may be used in any sequence and the fact that a party is conducting discovery, whether by deposition or otherwise, shall not operate to delay any other party's discovery.

(E) Supplementation of responses. A party who has responded to a request for discovery with a response that was complete when made is under no duty to supplement his response to include information thereafter acquired, except as follows:

(1) A party is under a duty seasonably to supplement his response with respect to any question directly addressed to:

(a) the identity and location of persons having knowledge of discoverable matters, and

(b) the identity of each person expected to be called as an expert witness at trial, the subject-matter on which he is expected to testify, and the substance of his testimony.

(2) A party is under a duty seasonably to amend a prior response if he obtains information upon the basis of which

(a) he knows that the response was incorrect when made, or

(b) he knows that the response though correct when made is no longer true and the circumstances are such that a failure to amend the response is in substance a knowing concealment.

(3) A duty to supplement responses may be imposed by order of the court, agreement of the parties, or at any time prior to trial through new requests for supplementation of prior responses.

(F) Informal Resolution of Discovery Disputes. Before any party files any motion or request to compel discovery pursuant to Rule 37, or any motion for protection from discovery pursuant to Rule 26(C), or any other discovery motion which seeks to enforce, modify, or limit discovery, that party shall:

(1) Make a reasonable effort to reach agreement with the opposing party concerning the matter which is the subject of the motion or request; and

(2) Include in the motion or request a statement showing that the attorney making the motion or request has made a reasonable effort to reach agreement with the opposing attorney(s) concerning the matter(s) set forth in the motion or request. This statement shall recite, in addition, the date, time and place of this effort to reach agreement, whether in person or by phone, and the names of all parties and attorneys participating therein. If an attorney for any party advises the court in writing that an opposing attorney has refused or delayed meeting and discussing the issues covered in this subsection (F), the court may take such action as is appropriate.

The court may deny a discovery motion filed by a party who has failed to comply with the requirements of this subsection.

Rule 27. Depositions before action or pending appeal

(A) Before action.

(1) Petition. A person who desires to perpetuate his own testimony or that of another person regarding any matter that may be cognizable in any court in which the action may be commenced, may file a verified petition in any such court of this state.

The petition shall be entitled in the name of the petitioner and shall state facts showing:

(a) that the petitioner expects to be a party to an action cognizable in a court of this or another state;

(b) the subject-matter of the expected action and his interest therein;

(c) the facts which he desires to establish by the proposed testimony and his reasons for desiring to perpetuate it;

(d) the names or a description of the persons he expects will be adverse parties and their addresses so far as known; and

(e) the names and addresses of the persons to be examined and the substance of the testimony which he expects to elicit from each, and shall ask for an order authorizing the petitioner to take the depositions of the persons to be examined named in the petition, for the purpose of perpetuating their testimony.

(2) Notice and service. The petitioner shall thereafter serve a notice upon each person named in the petition as an expected adverse party, together with a copy of the petition, stating that the petitioner will apply to the court, at a time and place named therein, for the order described in the petition. At least twenty [20] days before the date of hearing the notice shall be served in the manner provided in Rule 4 for service of summons; but if such service cannot with due diligence be made upon any expected adverse party named in the petition, the court may make such order as is just for service by publication or otherwise, and shall appoint, for persons not served in the manner provided in Rule 4, an attorney who shall represent them, and, in case they are not otherwise represented, shall cross-examine the deponent. If any expected adverse party is a minor or incompetent the provisions of Rule 17(C) apply.

(3) Order and examination. If the court is satisfied that the perpetuation of the testimony may prevent a failure or delay of justice, it shall make an order designating or describing the persons whose depositions may be taken and specifying the subject-matter of the examination or written interrogatories. The depositions may then be taken in accordance with these rules; and the court may make orders of the character provided for by Rules 34 and 35. For the purpose of applying these rules to depositions for perpetuating testimony, each reference therein to the court in which the action is pending shall be deemed to refer to the court in which the petition for such deposition was filed.

(4) Use of deposition. If a deposition to perpetuate testimony is taken under these rules or if, although not so taken, it would be admissible in evidence in the court of the state in which it is taken, it may be used in any action involving the same subject-matter subsequently brought in a court of this state in accordance with the provision of Rule 32.

(B) Pending appeal. If an appeal has been taken from a judgment of any court or before the taking of an appeal if the time therefor has not expired, the court in which the judgment was rendered may allow the taking of the depositions of witnesses to perpetuate their testimony for use in the event of further proceedings in such court. In such case the party who desires to perpetuate the testimony may make a motion in the court for leave to take the depositions, upon the same notice and service thereof as if the action was pending in the court. The motion shall show:

(1) the names and addresses of the persons to be examined and the substance of the testimony which he expects to elicit from each;

(2) the reasons for perpetuating their testimony.

If the court finds that the perpetuation of the testimony is proper to avoid a failure or delay of justice, it may make an order allowing the depositions to be taken and may make orders of the character provided for by Rules 34 and 35, and thereupon the depositions may be taken and used in the same manner and under the same conditions as are prescribed in these rules for depositions taken in actions pending in the court.

(C) Perpetuation by action. This rule does not limit the power of a court to entertain an action to perpetuate testimony.

(D) Filing deposition. The filing or custody of any deposition or evidence obtained under this rule shall be in accordance with Trial Rule 5(E).

Rule 28. Persons before whom depositions may be taken; discovery across state lines; before administrative agencies; and after judgment

(A) Within the United States. Within the United States or within a territory or insular possession subject to the dominion of the United States, depositions shall be taken before an officer authorized to administer oaths by the laws of the United States, or of the state of Indiana, or of the place where the examination is held, or before a person appointed by the court in which the action is pending. A person so appointed has power to administer oaths and take testimony.

(B) In foreign countries. In a foreign country, depositions may be taken:

(1) on notice before a person authorized to administer oaths in the place in which the examination is held, either by the law thereof or by the law of the United States; or

(2) before a person commissioned by the court, and a person so commissioned shall have the power by virtue of his commission to administer any necessary oath and take testimony; or

(3) pursuant to a letter rogatory.

A commission or a letter rogatory shall be issued on application and notice and on terms that are just and appropriate. It is not requisite to the issuance of a commission or a letter rogatory that the taking of the deposition in any other manner is impracticable or inconvenient; and both a commission and a letter rogatory may be issued in proper cases. A notice or commission may designate the person before whom the deposition is to be taken either by name or descriptive title. A letter rogatory may be addressed "To the Appropriate Authority in (here name the country)". Evidence obtained in response to a letter rogatory need not be excluded merely for the reason that it is not a verbatim transcript or that the testimony was not taken under oath or for any similar departure from the requirements for depositions taken within the United States under these rules.

(C) Disqualification for interest. Unless otherwise permitted by these rules, no deposition shall be taken before a person who is a relative or employee or attorney or counsel of any of the parties, or is a relative or employee of such attorney or counsel, or is financially interested in the action.

(D) Scope of discovery outside state--Protective and enforcement orders. A deposition may be taken outside the state as provided in subdivisions (A) and (B) of this rule, and the deponent may be requested to produce documents and things, and may also be requested to allow inspections and copies as provided in Rule 34 to submit to examination under Rule 35. Protective orders may be granted by the court in which the action is pending and by the court where discovery is being made. Enforcement orders may be made by the court where the discovery is sought, and enforcement orders and sanctions may be made by the court where the action is pending as against parties and as against witnesses subject to the jurisdiction of the court. When no action is pending, a court of this state may authorize a deposition to be taken outside this state of any person and upon any matters allowed by Rule 27.

(E) Assistance to tribunals and litigants outside this state. A court of this state may order a person who is domiciled or is found within this state to give his testimony or statement or to produce documents or other things, allow inspections and copies and permit physical and mental examinations for use in a proceeding in a tribunal outside this state. The order may be made upon the application of any interested person or in response to a letter rogatory and may prescribe the practice and procedure, which may be wholly or in part the practice and procedure of the tribunal outside this state, for taking the testimony or statement or producing the documents or other things. To the extent that the order does not prescribe otherwise, the practice and procedure shall be in accordance with that of the court of this state issuing the order. The order may direct that the testimony or statement be given, or document or other thing produced, before a person appointed by the court. The person appointed shall have power to administer any necessary oath. A person within this state may voluntarily give his testimony or statement or produce documents or other things allowing inspections and copies and permit physical and mental examinations for use in a proceeding before a tribunal outside this state

(F) Discovery proceedings before administrative agencies. Whenever an adjudicatory hearing, including any hearing in any proceeding subject to judicial review, is held by or before an administrative agency, any part to that adjudicatory hearing shall be entitled to use the discovery provisions of Rules 26 through 37 of the Indiana Rules of Trial Procedure. Such discovery may include any relevant matter in the custody and control of the administrative agency.

Protective and other orders shall be obtained first from the administrative agency, and if enforcement of such orders or right of discovery is necessary, it may be obtained in a court of general jurisdiction in the county wher discovery is being made or sought, or where the hearing is being held.

(G) Applicability of other laws. This rule does not repeal or modify any other law of this state permitting another procedure for obtaining discovery for use in this state or in a tribunal outside this state, except as expressly provided in these rules.

(H) Discovery after judgment. Discovery after judgment may be had in proceedings to enforce or to challenge the judgment.

Rule 29. Stipulations regarding discovery procedure

Unless the court orders otherwise, the parties may by written stipulation:

(1) provide that depositions may be taken before any person, at any time or place, upon any notice, and in any manner and when so taken may be used like other depositions, and

(2) modify the procedures provided by these rules for other methods of discovery.

Rule 30. Depositions Upon Oral Examination

(A) When depositions may be taken. After commencement of the action, any party may take the testimony of any person, including a party, by deposition upon oral examination. Leave of court, granted with or without notice, must be obtained only if the plaintiff seeks to take a deposition prior to the expiration of twenty [20] days after service of summons and complaint upon any defendant except that leave is not required:

(1) if a defendant has served a notice of taking deposition or otherwise sought discovery; or

(2) if special notice is given as provided in subdivision (B)(2) of this rule.

The attendance of witnesses may be compelled by the use of subpoena as provided in Rule 45. The deposition of a person confined in prison may be taken only by leave of court on such terms as the court prescribes.

(B) Notice of examination: General requirements--Special notice--Non-stenographic recording--Production of documents and things--Deposition of organization.

(1) A party desiring to take the deposition of any person upon oral examination shall give reasonable notice in writing to every other party to the action. The notice shall state the time and place for taking the deposition and the name and address of each person to be examined, if known, and if the name is not known, a general description sufficient to identify him or the particular class or group to which he belongs. If a subpoena duces tecum is to be served on the person to be examined, a designation of the materials to be produced thereunder shall be attached to or included in the notice.

(2) Leave of court, when required by subdivision (A) of this rule is not required for the taking of a deposition by plaintiff if the notice:

(a) states that the person to be examined is about to go out of the state or will be unavailable for examination unless his deposition is taken before expiration of the twenty [20] day period; and

(b) sets forth facts to support the statement.

The plaintiff's attorney shall sign the notice, and his signature constitutes a certification by him that to the best of his knowledge, information, and belief the statement and supporting facts are true. The sanctions provided by Rule 11 are applicable to the certification.

If any party shows that when he was served with notice under this subdivision (B)(2) he was unable through the exercise of diligence to obtain counsel to represent him at the taking of the deposition, the deposition may not be used against him.

(3) The court may for cause shown enlarge or shorten the time for taking the deposition.

(4) If a party taking a deposition wishes to have the testimony recorded other than in a manner provided in Rule 74, the notice shall specify the manner of recording and preserving the deposition. The court may require stenographic taking or make any other order to assure that the recorded testimony will be accurate and trustworthy.

(5) The notice to a deponent may be accompanied by a request made in compliance with Rule 34 for the production of documents and tangible things at the taking of the deposition.

(6) A party may in his notice name as the deponent an organization, including without limitation a governmental organization, or a partnership and designate with reasonable particularity the matters on which examination is requested. The organization so named shall designate one or more officers, directors, or managing agents, executive officers, or other persons duly authorized and consenting to testify on its behalf. The persons so designated shall testify as to matters known or available to the organization. This subdivision (B)(6) does not preclude taking a deposition by any other procedure authorized in these rules.

(C) Examination and cross-examination--Record of examination--Oath--Objections. Examination and cross-examination of witnesses may proceed as permitted at the trial under the provisions of Rule 43(B). The officer before whom the deposition is to be taken shall put the witness on oath and shall personally, or by someone acting under his direction and in his presence, record the testimony of the witness. The testimony shall be taken stenographically or recorded by any other means designated in accordance with subdivision (B)(4) of this rule. If requested by one of the parties, the testimony shall be transcribed.

All objections made at the time of the examination to the qualifications of the officer taking the deposition, or to the manner of taking it, or to the evidence presented, or to the conduct of any party, and any other objection to the proceedings, shall be noted by the officer upon the deposition. When there is an objection to a question, the objection and reason therefor shall be noted, and the question shall be answered unless the attorney instructs the deponent not to answer, or the deponent refuses to answer, in which case either party may have the question certified by the Reporter, and the question with the objection thereto when so certified shall be delivered to the party requesting the certification who may then proceed under Rule 37(A). In lieu of participating in the oral examination, parties may serve written questions on the party taking the deposition and require him to transmit them to the officer, who shall propound them to the witness and record the answers verbatim.

(D) Motion to terminate or limit examination. At any time during the taking of the deposition, on motion of any party or of the deponent and upon a showing that the examination is being conducted in bad faith or in such manner as unreasonably to annoy, embarrass, or oppress the deponent or party, the court in which the action is pending or the court in the county where the deposition is being taken may order the officer conducting the examination to cease forthwith from taking the deposition, or may limit the scope and manner of the taking of the deposition as provided in Rule 26(C). If the order made terminates the examination, it shall be resumed thereafter only upon the order of the court in which the action is pending. Upon demand of the objecting party or deponent the taking of the deposition shall be suspended for the time necessary to make a motion for an order. The provisions of Rule 37(A)(4) apply to the award of expenses incurred in relation to the motion.

(E) Submission to witness--Changes--Signing.

(1) When the testimony is fully transcribed, the deposition shall be submitted to the witness for reading and signing and shall be read to or by him, unless such reading and signing have been waived by the witness and by each party. "Submitted to the witness" as used in this subsection shall mean (a) mailing of written notification by registered or certified mail to the witness and each attorney attending the deposition that the deposition can be read and examined in the office of the officer before whom the deposition was taken, or (b), mailing the original deposition, by registered or certified mail, to the witness at an address designated by the witness or his attorney, if requested to do so by the witness, his attorney, or the party taking the deposition.

(2) If the witness desires to change any answer in the deposition submitted to him, each change, with a statement of the reason therefor, shall be made by the witness on a separate form provided by the officer, shall be signed by the witness and affixed to the original deposition by the officer. A copy of such changes shall be furnished by the officer to each party.

(3) If the reading and signing have not been waived by the witness and by each party the deposition shall be signed by the witness and returned by him to the officer within thirty (30) days after it is submitted to the witness. If the deposition has been returned to the officer and has not been signed by the witness, the officer shall execute a certificate of that fact, attach it to the original deposition and deliver it to the party taking it. In such event, the deposition may be used by any party with the same force and effect as though it had been signed by the witness.

(4) In the event the deposition is not returned to the officer within thirty (30) days after it has been submitted to the witness, the reporter shall execute a certificate of that fact and cause the certificate to be delivered t the party taking it. In such event, any party may use a copy of the deposition with the same force and effec as though the original had been signed by the witness.

(F) Certification and Filing--Exhibits—Copies.

(1) The officer shall certify on the deposition that the witness was duly sworn by him and that the deposition i a true record of the testimony given by the witness. He shall then securely seal the deposition in an envelope endorsed with the title of the action and marked "Deposition of (here insert name of witness)" and shall promptly deliver it to the party taking the deposition.

Documents and things, unless objection is made to their production for inspection during the examinatior of the witness, shall be marked for identification and annexed to and returned with the deposition, and may be inspected and copied by any party, except that:

(a) the person producing the materials may substitute copies to be marked for identification, if he afford to all parties fair opportunity to verify the copies by comparison with the originals; and

(b) if the person producing the materials requests their return the officer shall mark them, give each part an opportunity to inspect and copy them, and return them to the person producing them, and the materials may then be used in the same manner as if annexed to and returned with the deposition.

(2) Upon payment of reasonable charges therefor, the officer shall furnish a copy of the deposition to any part or the deponent.

(3) The officer taking the deposition shall give prompt notice to all parties of its delivery to the party taking th deposition.

(4) The filing of depositions shall be in accordance with the provisions of Trial Rule 5(E).

(G) Failure to attend or to serve subpoena--Expenses.

(1) If the party giving the notice of the taking of a deposition fails to attend and proceed therewith and anothe party attends in person or by attorney pursuant to the notice, the court may order the party giving the notice to pay to such other party the amount of the reasonable expenses incurred by him and his attorney in so attending, including reasonable attorney's fees.

(2) If the party giving the notice of the taking of a deposition of a witness other than a party fails to serve a subpoena upon him and the witness because of such failure does not attend, and if another party attends ir person or by attorney because he expects the deposition of that witness to be taken, the court may order th party giving the notice to pay to such other party the amount of the reasonable expenses incurred by him and his attorney in so attending, including reasonable attorney's fees.

Rule 31. Deposition of witnesses upon written questions

(A) Serving questions--Notice. After commencement of the action, any party may take the testimony of any person, including a party, by deposition upon written questions. The attendance of witnesses may be compelled by the use of subpoena as provided in Rule 45. The deposition of a person confined in prison may be taken only by leave of court on such terms as the court prescribes.

A party desiring to take a deposition upon written questions shall serve them upon every other party with a notice stating:

(1) the name and address of the person who is to answer them, if known, and if the name is not known, a general description sufficient to identify him or the particular class or group to which he belongs; and

(2) the name or descriptive title and address of the officer before whom the deposition is to be taken.

A deposition upon written questions may be taken of an organization, including a governmental organization, oı a partnership in accordance with the provisions of Rule 30(B)(6).

Within twenty [20] days after the notice and written questions are served, a party may serve cross questions upon all other parties. Within ten [10] days after being served with cross questions, a party may serve redirect questions upon all other parties. Within ten [10] days after being served with redirect questions, a party may serve recross questions upon all other parties. The court may for cause shown enlarge or shorten the time.

(B) Officer to take responses and prepare record. A copy of the notice and copies of all questions served shall be delivered by the party taking the deposition to the officer designated in the notice, who shall proceed promptly, in the manner provided by Rule 30(C), (E), and (F), to take the testimony of the witness in response to the questions and to prepare, certify, and deliver the deposition, attaching thereto the copy of the notice and the questions received by him, in accordance with Rule 5(E).

(C) Notice of filing. When the deposition is filed the party taking it shall promptly give notice thereof to all other parties.

Rule 32. Use of depositions in court proceedings

(A) Use of depositions. At the trial or upon the hearing of a motion or an interlocutory proceeding, any part or all of a deposition, so far as admissible under the Rules of Evidence applied as though the witness were then present and testifying, may be used against any party who was present or represented at the taking of the deposition, by or against any party who had reasonable notice thereof or by any party in whose favor it was given in accordance with any one [1] of the following provisions:

(1) Any deposition may be used by any party for the purpose of contradicting or impeaching the testimony of deponent as a witness.

(2) The deposition of a party, or an agent or person authorized by a party to testify or furnish such evidence or of anyone who at the time of taking the deposition was an officer, director, or managing agent, executive officer or a person designated under Rule 30(B)(6) or 31(A) to testify on behalf of an organization, including a governmental organization, or partnership which is a party may be used by an adverse party for any purpose.

(3) The deposition of a witness, whether or not a party, may be used by any party for any purpose if the court finds:

(a) that the witness is dead; or

(b) that the witness is outside the state, unless it appears that the absence of the witness was procured by the party offering the deposition; or

(c) that the witness is unable to attend or testify because of age, sickness, infirmity, or imprisonment; or

(d) that the party offering the deposition has been unable to procure the attendance of the witness by subpoena; or

(e) upon application and notice, that such exceptional circumstances exist as to make it desirable, in the interest of justice and with due regard to the importance of presenting the testimony of witnesses orally in open court, to allow the deposition to be used; or

(f) upon agreement of the parties.

(4) If only part of a deposition is offered in evidence by a party, an adverse party may require him to introduce any other part which ought in context to be considered with the part introduced, and any party may introduce any other parts.

Substitution of parties pursuant to Rule 25 does not affect the right to use depositions previously taken; and, when an action in any court of the United States or of any state has been dismissed and another action involving the same subject-matter is afterward brought between the same parties or their representatives or successors in interest, all depositions lawfully taken and duly filed in the former action may be used in the latter as if originally taken therefor.

(B) Objections to admissibility. Subject to the provisions of Rule 28(B) and subdivision (D)(3) of this rule, objection may be made at the trial or hearing to receiving in evidence any depositions or part thereof for any reason which would require the exclusion of the evidence if the witness were then present and testifying.

(C) Effect of taking or using depositions. A party does not make a person his own witness for any purpose by taking his deposition. The introduction in evidence of the deposition or any part thereof for any purpose other than that of contradicting or impeaching the deponent makes the deponent the witness of the party introducing the deposition, but this shall not apply to the use by an adverse party of a deposition as described in subdivision (A)(2) of this rule. At the trial or hearing any party may rebut any relevant evidence contained in a deposition whether introduced by him or by any other party.

(D) Effect of errors and irregularities in depositions.

(1) As to notice. All errors and irregularities in the notice for taking a deposition are waived unless written objection is promptly served upon the party giving the notice.

(2) As to disqualification of officer. Objection to taking a deposition because of disqualification of the officer before whom it is to be taken is waived unless made before the taking of the deposition begins or as soon thereafter as the disqualification becomes known or could be discovered with reasonable diligence.

(3) As to taking of deposition.

(a) Objections to the competency of a witness or to the competency, relevancy, or materiality of testimony are not waived by failure to make them before or during the taking of the deposition, unless the ground of the objection is one which might have been obviated or removed if presented at that time.

(b) Errors and irregularities occurring at the oral examination in the manner of taking the deposition, in the form of the questions or answers, in the oath or affirmation, or in the conduct of parties and error of any kind which might be obviated, removed, or cured if promptly presented, are waived unless reasonable objection thereto is made at the taking of the deposition.

(c) Objections to the form of written questions submitted under Rule 31 are waived unless served in writing upon the party propounding them within the time allowed for serving the succeeding cross or other questions and within five [5] days after service of the last questions authorized.

(4) As to completion and return of deposition. Errors and irregularities in the manner in which the testimony is transcribed or the deposition is prepared, signed, certified, sealed, indorsed, transmitted, filed, or otherwise dealt with by the officer under Rules 30 and 31 are waived unless a motion to suppress the deposition or some part thereof is made with reasonable promptness after such defect is, or with due diligence might have been, ascertained.

Rule 33. Interrogatories to Parties

(A) Availability--Procedures for use. Any party may serve upon any other party written interrogatories to be answered by the party served or, if the party served is an organization including a governmental organization, or a partnership, by any officer or agent, who shall furnish such information as is available to the party. Interrogatories may, without leave of court, be served upon the plaintiff after commencement of the action and upon any other party with or after service of the summons and complaint upon that party.

(B) Format of interrogatory and response. A party who serves written interrogatories under this rule shall provide, after each interrogatory, a reasonable amount of space for a response or an objection. Answers or objections to interrogatories shall include the interrogatory which is being answered or to which an objection is made. The interrogatory which is being answered or objected to shall be placed immediately preceding the answer or objection.

Each interrogatory shall be answered separately and fully in writing under oath, unless it is objected to, in which event the reasons for objections shall be stated in lieu of an answer. The answers are to be signed by the person making them, and the objections signed by the attorney making them.

(C) Time for service, response, and sanctions. The party upon whom the interrogatories have been served shall serve a copy of the answers and objections within a period designated by the party submitting the interrogatories, not less than thirty (30) days after the service thereof or within such shorter or longer time as the court may allow. The party submitting the interrogatories may move for an order under Rule 37(A) with respect to any objection to or other failure to answer an interrogatory.

The party upon whom the interrogatories have been served may object to the failure to follow the Format requirements in subpart (B) by returning the interrogatories to the party who caused them to be served. If this objection is to be made, the interrogatories shall be returned to the party who caused them to be served not later than the seventh (7th) day after they were received. If the interrogatories are not returned in that time, then this objection is waived.

(D) Scope--Use at trial. Interrogatories may relate to any matters which can be inquired into under Rule 26(B), and the answers may be used to the extent permitted by the rules of evidence.

An interrogatory otherwise proper is not objectionable merely because an answer to the interrogatory involves an opinion, contention, or legal conclusion, but the court may order that such an interrogatory be answered at a later time, or after designated discovery has been completed, or at a pre-trial conference.

(E) Option to produce business records. Where the answer to an interrogatory may be derived or ascertained from the business records of the party upon whom the interrogatory has been served or from an examination, audit or inspection of such business records, including a compilation, abstract or summary thereof, and the burden of deriving or ascertaining the answer is substantially the same for the party serving the interrogatory as for the party served, it is a sufficient answer to such interrogatory to specify the records from which the answer may be derived or ascertained and to afford to the party serving the interrogatory reasonable opportunity to examine, audit or inspect such records and to make copies, compilations, abstracts or summaries. A specification shall be in sufficient detail to permit the interrogating party to locate and to identify, as readily as can the party served, the records from which the answer may be ascertained.

ule 34. Production of documents, electronically stored information, and things and entry upon land for ıspection and other purposes

(A) Scope. Any party may serve on any other party a request:

(1) to produce and permit the party making the request, or someone acting on the requester's behalf, to inspect and copy, any designated documents or electronically stored information (including, without limitation, writings, drawings, graphs, charts, photographs, sound recordings, images and other data or data compilations from which information can be obtained or translated, if necessary, by the respondent into reasonably usable form) or to inspect and copy, test, or sample any designated tangible things which constitute or contain matters within the scope of Rule 26(B) and which are in the possession, custody or control of the party upon whom the request is served; or

(2) to permit entry upon designated land or other property in the possession or control of the party upon whom the request is served for the purpose of inspection and measuring, surveying, photographing, testing, or sampling the property or any designated object or operation thereon, within the scope of Rule 26(B).

(B) Procedure. The request may, without leave of court, be served upon the plaintiff after commencement of the action and upon any other party with or after service of the summons and complaint upon that party. The request shall set forth the items to be inspected either by individual item or by category, and describe each item and category with reasonable particularity. The request may specify the form or forms in which electronically stored information is to be produced. The request shall specify a reasonable time, place, and manner of making the inspection and performing the related acts. Service is dispensed with if the whereabouts of the parties is unknown.

The party upon whom the request is served shall serve a written response within a period designated in the request, not less than thirty [30] days after the service thereof or within such shorter or longer time as the court may allow. The response shall state, with respect to each item or category, that inspection and related activities will be permitted as requested, unless it is objected to, including an objection to the requested form or forms for producing electronically stored information, stating in which event the reasons for objection shall be stated. If objection is made to part of an item or category, the part shall be specified. If objection is made to the requested form or forms for producing electronically stored information--or if no form was specified in the request--the responding party must state the form or forms it intends to use. The party submitting the request may move for an order under Rule 37(A) with respect to any objection to or other failure to respond to the request or any part thereof, or any failure to permit inspection as requested.

Unless the parties otherwise agree, or the court otherwise orders, a party who produces documents for inspection shall produce them as they are kept in the usual course of business or shall organize and label them to correspond with the categories in the request.

If a request for electronically stored information does not specify the form or forms of production, a responding party must produce the information in a form or forms in which it is ordinarily maintained or in a form or forms that are reasonably usable.

A party need not produce the same electronically stored information in more than one form.

(C) Application to Non-parties:

(1) A witness or person other than a party may be requested to produce or permit the matters allowed by subsection (A) of this rule. Such request shall be served upon other parties and included in or with a subpoena served upon such witness or person.

(2) Neither a request nor subpoena to produce or permit as permitted by this rule shall be served upon a non-party until at least fifteen (15) days after the date on which the party intending to serve such request or subpoena serves a copy of the proposed request and subpoena on all other parties. Provided, however, that if such request or subpoena relates to a matter set for hearing within such fifteen (15) day period or arises out of a bona fide emergency, such request or subpoena may be served upon a non-party one (1) day after receipt of the proposed request or subpoena by all other parties.

(3) The request shall contain the matter provided in subsection (B) of this rule. It shall also state that the witness or person to whom it is directed is entitled to security against damages or payment of damages resulting from such request and may respond to such request by submitting to its terms, by proposing different terms, by objecting specifically or generally to the request by serving a written response to the party making the request within thirty (30) days, or by moving to quash as permitted by Rule 45(B). Any party, or any witness or person upon whom the request properly is made may respond to the request as provided in subsection (B) of this rule. If the response of the witness or person to whom it is directed is unfavorable, if he moves to quash, if he refuses to cooperate after responding or fails to respond, or if he

objects, the party making the request may move for an order under Rule 37(A) with respect to any such response or objection. In granting an order under this subsection and Rule 37(A)(2) the court shall condition relief upon the prepayment of damages to be proximately incurred by the witness or person to whom the request is directed or require an adequate surety bond or other indemnity conditioned against such damages. Such damages shall include reasonable attorneys' fees incurred in reasonable resistance an in establishing such threatened damage or damages.

(4) A party receiving documents from a non-party pursuant to this provision shall serve copies on all other parties within fifteen (15) days of receiving the documents. If the documents are voluminous and service o a complete set of copies is burdensome, the receiving party shall notify all parties within fifteen (15) days o receiving the documents that the documents are available for inspection at the location of their production by the non-party, or at another location agreed to by the parties. The parties shall agree to arrangements for copying, and any party desiring copies shall bear the cost of reproducing them.

(D) Exception to best evidence rule. When a party or witness in control of a writing or document subject to examination under this rule or Rule 9.2(E) refuses or is unable to produce it, evidence thereof shall be allowed by other parties without compliance with the rule of evidence requiring production of the original document or writing as best evidence.

Rule 35. Physical and mental examination of persons

(A) Order for examination. When the mental or physical condition (including the blood group) of a party, or of person in the custody or under the legal control of a party, is in controversy, the court in which the action is pending may order the party to submit to a physical or mental examination by a suitably licensed or certified examiner or to produce for examination the person in his custody or legal control. The order may be made only on motion for good cause shown and upon notice to the person to be examined and to all parties and shall specify the time, place, manner, conditions, and scope of the examination and the person or persons by whom it is to be made.

(B) Report of licensed or certified examiner.

(1) If requested by the party against whom an order is made under Rule 35(A) or the person examined, the party causing the examination to be made shall deliver to him a copy of a detailed written report of the examiner setting out his findings, including results of all tests made, diagnoses and conclusions, together with like reports of all earlier examinations of the same condition. After delivery the party causing the examination shall be entitled upon request to receive from the party against whom the order is made a like report of any examination, previously or thereafter made, of the same condition, unless, in the case of a report of examination of a person not a party, the party shows that he is unable to obtain it. The court on motion may make an order against a party requiring delivery of a report on such terms as are just, and if an examiner fails or refuses to make a report the court may exclude his testimony if offered at the trial.

(2) By requesting and obtaining a report of the examination so ordered or by taking the deposition of the examiner, the party examined waives any privilege he may have in that action or any other involving the same controversy, regarding the testimony of every other person who has examined or may thereafter examine him in respect of the same mental or physical condition.

(3) This subdivision applies to examinations made by agreement of the parties, unless the agreement expressly provides otherwise. This subdivision does not preclude discovery of a report of an examiner or the taking of a deposition of the examiner in accordance with the provisions of any other rule.

Rule 36. Requests for admission

(A) Request for admission. A party may serve upon any other party a written request for the admission, for purposes of the pending action only, of the truth of any matters within the scope of Rule 26(B) set forth in the request, including the genuineness of any documents described in the request. Copies of documents shall be served with the request unless they have been or are otherwise furnished or made available for inspection and copying. The request may, without leave of court, be served upon the plaintiff after commencement of the action and upon any other party with or after service of the summons and complaint upon that party.

Each matter of which an admission is requested shall be separately set forth. The matter is admitted unless, within a period designated in the request, not less than thirty [30] days after service thereof or within such shorter or longer time as the court may allow, the party to whom the request is directed serves upon the party requesting the admission a written answer or objection addressed to the matter, signed by the party or by his attorney. If objection is made, the reasons therefor shall be stated. The answer shall specifically deny the matter or set forth in detail the reasons why the answering party cannot truthfully admit or deny the matter. A denial shall fairly meet the substance of the requested admission, and when good faith requires that a party qualify his answer or deny only a part of the matter of which an admission is requested, he shall specify so much of it as is true and qualify or deny the remainder. An answering party may not give lack of information or knowledge as a reason for failure to admit or deny unless he states that he has made reasonable inquiry and that the information known or readily obtainable by him is insufficient to enable him to admit or deny or that the inquiry would be unreasonably burdensome. A party who considers that a matter of which an admission has been requested presents a genuine issue for trial may not, on that ground alone, object to the request; he may, subject to the provisions of Rule 37(C), deny the matter or set forth reasons why he cannot admit or deny it.

The party who has requested the admissions may move for an order with respect to the answers or objections. Unless the court determines that an objection is justified, it shall order that an answer be served. If the court determines that an answer does not comply with the requirements of this rule, it may order either that the matter is admitted or that an amended answer be served. The court may, in lieu of these orders, determine that final disposition of the request be made at a pre-trial conference or at a designated time prior to trial. The provisions of Rule 37(A)(4) apply to the award of expenses incurred in relation to the motion.

(B) Effect of admission. Any matter admitted under this rule is conclusively established unless the court on motion permits withdrawal or amendment of the admission. Subject to the provisions of Rule 16 governing amendment of a pre-trial order, the court may permit withdrawal or amendment when the presentation of the merits of the action will be subserved thereby and the party who obtained the admission fails to satisfy the court that withdrawal or amendment will prejudice him in maintaining his action or defense on the merits. Any admission made by a party under this rule is for the purpose of the pending action only and is not an admission by him for any other purpose nor may it be used against him in any other proceeding.

Rule 37. Failure to make or cooperate in discovery: Sanctions

(A) Motion for order compelling discovery. A party, upon reasonable notice to other parties and all persons affected thereby, may apply for an order compelling discovery as follows:

(1) Appropriate court. An application for an order to a party may be made to the court in which the action is pending, or alternately, on matters relating to a deposition or an order under Rule 34, to the court in the county where the deposition is being taken or where compliance is to be made under Rule 34. An application for an order to a deponent who is not a party shall be made to the court in the county where the deposition is being taken.

(2) Motion. If a party refuses to allow inspection under Rule 9.2(E), or if a deponent fails to answer a question propounded or submitted under Rule 30 or 31, or an organization, including without limitation a governmental organization or a partnership, fails to make designation under Rule 30(B)(6) or 31(A), or a party fails to answer an interrogatory submitted under Rule 33, or if a party or witness or other person, in response to a request submitted under Rule 34, fails to respond that inspection will be permitted as requested or fails to permit inspection as requested, the discovering party may move for an order compelling an answer, or a designation, or an order compelling inspection in accordance with the request. When taking a deposition on oral examination, the proponent of the question may complete or adjourn the examination before he applies for an order.

If the court denies the motion in whole or in part, it may make such protective order as it would have been empowered to make on a motion made pursuant to Rule 26(C).

(3) Evasive or incomplete answer. For purposes of this subdivision an evasive or incomplete answer is to be treated as a failure to answer.

(4) Award of expenses of motion. If the motion is granted, the court shall, after opportunity for hearing, require the party or deponent whose conduct necessitated the motion or the party or attorney advising such conduct or both of them to pay to the moving party the reasonable expenses incurred in obtaining the order, including attorney's fees, unless the court finds that the opposition to the motion was substantially justified or that other circumstances make an award of expenses unjust.

If the motion is denied, the court shall, after opportunity for hearing, require the moving party or the attorney advising the motion or both of them to pay to the party or deponent who opposed the motion the reasonable expenses incurred in opposing the motion, including attorney's fees, unless the court finds that the making of the motion was substantially justified or that other circumstances make an award of expenses unjust.

If the motion is granted in part and denied in part, the court may apportion the reasonable expenses incurred in relation to the motion among the parties and persons in a just manner.

(B) Failure to comply with order.

(1) Sanctions by court in county where deposition is taken. If a deponent fails to be sworn or to answer a question after being directed to do so by the court in the county in which the deposition is being taken, the failure may be considered a contempt of that court.

(2) Sanctions by court in which action is pending. If a party or an officer, director, or managing agent of a party or an organization, including a governmental organization, or a person designated under Rule 30(B)(6) or 31(A) to testify on behalf of a party or an organization, including a governmental organization, fails to obey an order to provide or permit discovery, including an order made under subdivision (A) of this rule or Rule 35, the court in which the action is pending may make such orders in regard to the failure as are just, and among others the following:

  (a) An order that the matters regarding which the order was made or any other designated facts shall be taken to be established for the purposes of the action in accordance with the claim of the party obtaining the order;

  (b) An order refusing to allow the disobedient party to support or oppose designated claims or defenses, or prohibiting him from introducing designated matters in evidence;

  (c) An order striking out pleadings or parts thereof, or staying further proceedings until the order is obeyed, or dismissing the action or proceeding or any part thereof, or rendering a judgment by default against the disobedient party;

  (d) In lieu of any of the foregoing orders or in addition thereto, an order treating as a contempt of court the failure to obey any orders except an order to submit to a physical or mental examination under Rule 35;

  (e) Where a party has failed to comply with an order under Rule 35(A) requiring him to produce another for examination, such orders as are listed in paragraphs (a), (b), and (c) of this subdivision, unless the party failing to comply shows that he is unable to produce such person for examination.

In lieu of any of the foregoing orders or in addition thereto, the court shall require the party failing to obey the order or the attorney advising him or both to pay the reasonable expenses, including attorney's fees, caused by the failure, unless the court finds that the failure was substantially justified or that other circumstances make an award of expenses unjust.

(C) Expenses on failure to admit.

If a party fails to admit the genuineness of any document or the truth of any matter as requested under Rule 36, and if the party requesting the admissions thereafter proves the genuineness of the document or the truth of the matter, he may apply to the court for an order requiring the other party to pay him the reasonable expenses incurred in making that proof, including reasonable attorney's fees. The court shall make the order unless it finds that (1) the request was held objectionable pursuant to Rule 36(A), or (2) the admission sought was of no substantial importance, or (3) the party failing to admit had reasonable ground to believe that he might prevail on the matter, or (4) there was other good reason for the failure to admit.

(D) Failure of party to attend at own deposition or serve answers to interrogatories or respond to requests for inspection.

If a party or an officer, director, or managing agent of a party or an organization, including without limitation a governmental organization, or a person designated under Rule 30(B)(6) or 31(A) to testify on behalf of a party or an organization, including without limitation a governmental organization, fails (1) to appear before the officer who is to take his deposition, after being served with a proper notice, or (2) to serve answers or objections to interrogatories submitted under Rule 33, after proper service of the interrogatories, or (3) to serve a written response to a request for inspection submitted under Rule 34, after proper service of the request, the court in which the action is pending on motion may make such orders in regard to the failure as are just, and among others it may take any action authorized under paragraphs (a), (b), and (c) of subdivision (B)(2) of this rule. In lieu of any order or in addition thereto, the court shall require the party failing to act or the attorney advising him or both to pay the reasonable expenses, including attorney's fees, caused by the failure, unless the court finds that the failure was substantially justified or that other circumstances make an award of expenses unjust.

The failure to act described in this subdivision may not be excused on the ground that the discovery sought is objectionable unless the party failing to act has applied for a protective order as provided by Rule 26(C).

(E) Electronically stored information. Absent exceptional circumstances, a court may not impose sanctions under these rules on a party for failing to provide electronically stored information lost as a result of the routine, good faith operation of an electronic information system.

Rule 38. Jury Trial of Right

(A) Causes triable by court and by jury. Issues of law and issues of fact in causes that prior to the eighteenth day of June, 1852, were of exclusive equitable jurisdiction shall be tried by the court; issues of fact in all other causes shall be triable as the same are now triable. In case of the joinder of causes of action or defenses which, prior to said date, were of exclusive equitable jurisdiction with causes of action or defenses which, prior to said date, were designated as actions at law and triable by jury--the former shall be triable by the court, and the latter by a jury, unless waived; the trial of both may be at the same time or at different times, as the court may direct.

(B) Demand. Any party may demand a trial by jury of any issue triable of right by a jury by filing with the court and serving upon the other parties a demand therefor in writing at any time after the commencement of the action and not later than ten (10) days after the first responsive pleading to the complaint, or to a counterclaim, crossclaim or other claim if one properly is pleaded; and if no responsive pleading is filed or required, within ten (10) days after the time such pleading otherwise would have been required. Such demand is sufficient if indorsed upon a pleading of a party filed within such time.

(C) Same: Specification of issues. In his demand a party may specify the issues which he wishes so tried; otherwise he shall be deemed to have demanded trial by jury for all issues triable as of right by jury. Any other party must file a demand for jury trial to preserve his right to trial by jury:

(1) of issues for which a right to trial by jury was not requested by another party; and

(2) in case a request by another party was improper. But if a proper request for a trial by jury upon issues triable by jury as of right on his behalf is made by any party, such request shall be deemed to have been made on behalf of all parties entitled to a jury trial upon such issues.

(D) Waiver. The failure of a party to appear at the trial, and the failure of a party to serve a demand as required by this rule and to file it as required by Rule 5(E) constitute waiver by him of trial by jury. A demand for trial by jury made as herein provided may not be withdrawn without the consent of the other party or parties.

The trial court shall not grant a demand for a trial by jury filed after the time fixed in T.R. 38(B) has elapsed except upon the written agreement of all of the parties to the action, which agreement shall be filed with the court and made a part of the record. If such agreement is filed then the court may, in its discretion, grant a trial by jury in which event the grant of a trial by jury may not be withdrawn except by the agreement of all of the parties.

(E) Arbitration. Nothing in these rules shall deny the parties the right by contract or agreement to submit or to agree to submit controversies to arbitration made before or after commencement of an action thereon or deny the courts power to specifically enforce such agreements.

Rule 39. Trial by jury or by the court

(A) By jury. When trial by jury has been demanded as provided in Rule 38, the action shall be designated in the Chronological Case Summary as a jury action. Issues upon which a jury trial is so demanded shall be tried by jury, subject to the following exceptions:

(1) If the parties or their attorneys of record, by written stipulation filed with the court or by oral stipulation made in open court and entered in the record, consent to trial by the court sitting without a jury upon any or all issues triable by jury as of right and so demanded, the court shall try those issues without a jury. The stipulation shall be effective only if filed or made in court before evidence is admitted at the trial or at such later time as the court, in its discretion, may allow.

(2) If a party demands a jury trial on any issue upon which he is entitled to jury trial as of right in the case, the court shall grant it on that issue.

(B) By the court--Advisory jury--Trial by consent. In any case where there are issues upon which a jury trial has not been demanded or has not properly been demanded or upon which there is no right to trial by jury as of right, the court may submit any or all of such issues to a jury for trial. The verdict shall be advisory unless, before the jury retires, the court, with the consent of both parties or their attorneys, orders that the verdict shall have the same effect as if a trial by jury had been a matter of right. Such order shall be granted at the court's discretion, and all issues shall be tried as if subject to jury trial as a matter of right unless the parties' consent is limited to fewer issues, or unless the court limits its order to fewer of those issues upon which consent has been given.

(C) Rulings of the court--Objections. In proceeding under Rules 38 and 39, error may be predicated upon the court's ruling or action without motion or other objection by a party.

(D) Findings in case of advisory jury. Findings of fact shall not be required upon issues to the extent that the judge's decision follows the verdict of a properly selected advisory jury.

Rule 40. Assignment of cases for trial

(A) [FN1] **Rules for assignment of cases.** The trial courts shall provide by rule for placing of actions upon the trial calendar:

(1) without request of the parties; or

(2) upon request of a party and notice to the other parties; or

(3) in such manner as the court determines will expedite trials.

Precedence shall be given to actions entitled thereto by any statute of the state, including hearings upon temporary restraining orders, injunctions and receiverships.

[FN1] This rule contains no subd. (B).

Rule 41. Dismissal of actions

(A) Voluntary dismissal: Effect thereof.

(1) By plaintiff--By stipulation. Subject to contrary provisions of these rules or of any statute, an action may be dismissed by the plaintiff without order of court:

(a) by filing a notice of dismissal at any time before service by the adverse party of an answer or of a motion for summary judgment, whichever first occurs; or

(b) by filing a stipulation of dismissal signed by all parties who have appeared in the action.

Unless otherwise stated in the notice of dismissal or stipulation, the dismissal is without prejudice, except that a notice of dismissal operates as an adjudication upon the merits when filed by a plaintiff who has once dismissed in any court of the United States or of any state an action based on or including the same claim. The provisions of this subdivision shall not apply if the plaintiff in such action could not effectuate service of process, or otherwise procure adjudication on the merits.

(2) By order of court. Except as provided in subsection (1) of this subdivision of this rule, an action shall not be dismissed at the plaintiff's instance save upon order of the court and upon such terms and conditions as the court deems proper. If a counterclaim or cross-claim has been pleaded by a defendant prior to the service upon him of the plaintiff's motion to dismiss, the action shall not be dismissed against the defendant's objection unless the counterclaim or cross-claim can remain pending for independent adjudication by the court. Unless otherwise specified in the order, a dismissal under this subsection is without prejudice.

(B) Involuntary dismissal: Effect thereof. After the plaintiff or party with the burden of proof upon an issue, in an action tried by the court without a jury, has completed the presentation of his evidence thereon, the opposing party, without waiving his right to offer evidence in the event the motion is not granted, may move for a dismissal on the ground that upon the weight of the evidence and the law there has been shown no right to relief. The court as trier of the facts may then determine them and render judgment against the plaintiff or may decline to render any judgment until the close of all the evidence. If the court renders judgment on the merits against the plaintiff or party with the burden of proof, the court, when requested at the time of the motion by either party shall make findings if, and as required by Rule 52(A). Unless the court in its order for dismissal otherwise specifies, a dismissal under this subdivision or subdivision (E) of this rule and any dismissal not provided for in this rule, other than a dismissal for lack of jurisdiction, operates as an adjudication upon the merits.

(C) Dismissal of counterclaim, cross-claim, or third-party claim. The provisions of this rule apply to the dismissal of any counterclaim, cross-claim, or third-party claim. A voluntary dismissal by the claimant alone pursuant to subsection (1) of subdivision (A) of this rule shall be made before a responsive pleading is served or, if there is none, before the introduction of evidence at the trial or hearing.

(D) Costs of previously-dismissed action. If a plaintiff who has once dismissed an action in any court commences an action based upon or including the same claim against the same defendant, the court may make such order for the payment of costs of the action previously dismissed as it may deem proper and may stay the proceedings in the action until the plaintiff has complied with the order.

(E) Failure to prosecute civil actions or comply with rules. Whenever there has been a failure to comply with these rules or when no action has been taken in a civil case for a period of sixty [60] days, the court, on motion of a party or on its own motion shall order a hearing for the purpose of dismissing such case. The court shall enter an order of dismissal at plaintiff's costs if the plaintiff shall not show sufficient cause at or before such hearing. Dismissal may be withheld or reinstatement of dismissal may be made subject to the condition that the plaintiff comply with these rules and diligently prosecute the action and upon such terms that the court in its discretion determines to be necessary to assure such diligent prosecution.

(F) Reinstatement following dismissal. For good cause shown and within a reasonable time the court may set aside a dismissal without prejudice. A dismissal with prejudice may be set aside by the court for the grounds and in accordance with the provisions of Rule 60(B).

Rule 42. Consolidation--Separate trials

(A) Consolidation. When actions involving a common question of law or fact are pending before the court, it may order a joint hearing or trial of any or all the matters in issue in the actions; it may order all the actions consolidated; and it may make such orders concerning proceedings therein as may tend to avoid unnecessary costs or delay.

(B) Separate trials. The court, in furtherance of convenience or to avoid prejudice, or when separate trials will be conducive to expedition and economy, may order a separate trial of any claim, cross-claim, counterclaim, or third-party claim, or of any separate issue or of any number of claims, cross-claims, counterclaims, third-party claims, or issues, always preserving inviolate the right of trial by jury.

(C) Submission to Jury in Stages. The Court upon its own motion or the motion of any party for good cause shown may allow the case to be tried and submitted to the jury in stages or segments including, but not limited to, bifurcation of claims or issues of compensatory and punitive damages.

(D) Actions Pending in Different Courts. When civil actions involving a common question of law or fact are pending in different courts, a party to any of the actions may, by motion, request consolidation of those actions for the purpose of discovery and any pre-trial proceedings. Such motion may only be filed in the court having jurisdiction of the action with the earliest filing date and the court shall enter an order of consolidation for the purpose of discovery and any pre-trial proceedings unless good cause to the contrary is shown and found by the court to exist. In the event two or more actions have the same earliest filing date, the motion may be filed only in the court having the lowest court identifier number under Administrative Rule 8(B)(1), which court shall be considered as having the action with the earliest filing date. Upon completion of discovery and any pre-trial proceedings, each case which has been subject to the order of consolidation shall be ordered returned to the court in which it was pending at the time the order of consolidation was made unless, after notice to all parties and a hearing, the court finds that the action involves unusual or complicated issues of fact or law or involves a substantial question of law of great public importance. In the event the court makes such a finding, it may enter an order of consolidation for the purpose of trial. Except for cause pursuant to IC 34-35-1-1, the right to a change of venue in any action consolidated under this rule shall be suspended during the period of consolidation. Such right shall be reinstated on entry of an order remanding the action to the court in which it was pending at the time of consolidation and the time prescribed for the filing of a motion for change of venue shall be deemed tolled during the period of suspension. Nothing in this Rule shall restrict the equitable discretion of the court having the earliest filed action to dismiss or stay that action. If such an order is entered, that court shall no longer be considered the court in which is pending the action with the earliest filing date for purposes of this Rule. This Subsection (D) shall not apply to actions pending in courts of limited jurisdiction and no such action may be consolidated with another under the provisions of this Subsection (D).

Rule 43. Evidence

(A) Form and admissibility. In all trials the testimony of witnesses shall be taken in open court, unless state law, these rules, the Indiana Rules of Evidence, or other rules adopted by the Indiana Supreme Court provide otherwise.

(B) Evidence on motions. When a motion is based on facts not appearing of record the court may hear the matter on affidavits presented by the respective parties, but the court may direct that the matter be heard wholly or partly on oral testimony or depositions.

(C) Interpreters. The court may appoint an interpreter of its own selection and may fix his reasonable compensation. The compensation shall be paid out of funds provided by law or by one or more of the parties as the court may direct, and may be taxed ultimately as costs, in the discretion of the court. Application of this rule shall be in compliance with the Americans with Disabilities Act.

(D) How evidence is presented. The trial shall proceed in the following order, unless the court within its discretion, otherwise directs: First, the party upon whom rests the burden of the issues may briefly state his case and the evidence by which he expects to sustain it. Second, the adverse party may then briefly state his defense and the evidence he expects to offer in support of it. Third, the party on whom rests the burden of the issues must first produce his evidence thereon; the adverse party will then produce his evidence which may then be rebutted.

(E) Public Access. Court Records filed or introduced in court proceedings are not confidential except to the extent provided by Administrative Rule 9(G).

Rule 44. Proof of official record

The rules concerning proof of official records are governed by the Rules of Evidence.

Rule 44.1. Determination of foreign law

(A) Foreign law. A party who intends to raise an issue concerning the law of a foreign country shall give notice in his pleadings or other reasonable written notice. The court, in determining foreign law, may consider any relevant material or source, including testimony, whether or not submitted by a party or admissible under Rule 43. The court's determination shall be treated as a ruling on a question of law. It shall be made by the court and not the jury and shall be reviewable.

(B) Law of other states and territories. Judicial notice, proof and notice of intent to offer evidence of the law o another jurisdiction not covered by subdivision (A) of this rule shall be governed by the Uniform Judicial Notice of Foreign Law Act, 1937 Indiana Acts, ch. 124 [FN1].

[FN1] IC 34-3-2-1 to 34-3-2-7, repealed in 1998.

Rule 45. Subpoena

(A) For Attendance of Witnesses--Form--Issuance.

(1) Every subpoena shall:

(a) state the name of the court;

(b) state the title of the action (without naming more than the first named plaintiffs and defendants in the complaint and the case number); and

(c) command each person to whom it is directed to attend and give testimony at a time and place therein specified.

(2) The clerk shall issue a subpoena, or a subpoena for the production of documentary evidence, signed and sealed but otherwise in blank, to a party requesting it or his or her attorney, who shall fill it in before service. An attorney admitted to practice law in this state, as an officer of the court, may also issue and sign such subpoena on behalf of (a) a court in which the attorney has appeared for a party; or (b) a court in which a deposition or production is compelled by the subpoena, if the deposition or production pertains to an action pending in a court where the attorney has appeared for a party in that case.

(B) For production of documentary evidence. A subpoena may also command the person to whom it is directed to produce the books, papers, documents, or tangible things designated therein; but the court, upon motion made promptly and in any event at or before the time specified in the subpoena for compliance therewith, may

(1) quash or modify the subpoena if it is unreasonable and oppressive or

(2) condition denial of the motion upon the advancement by the person in whose behalf the subpoena is issued of the reasonable cost of producing the books, papers, documents, or tangible things.

(C) Service. A subpoena may be served by the sheriff or his deputy, a party or any person. Service of a subpoena upon a person named therein shall be made by delivering a copy thereof to such person. Service may be made in the same manner as provided in Rule 4.1, Rule 4.16 and Rule 5(B).

(D) Subpoena for taking depositions--Place of examination.

(1) Proof of service of a notice to take a deposition as provided in Rules 30(B) and 31(A) constitutes a sufficient authorization for the issuance by the clerk of court for the county in which the deposition is to be taken of subpoenas for the persons named or described therein. The subpoena may command the person to whom it is directed to produce designated books, papers, documents, or tangible things which constitute or contain matters within the scope of the examination permitted by Rule 26(B), but in that event the subpoena will be subject to the provisions of Rule 26(C) and subdivision (B) of this rule.

(2) An individual may be required to attend an examination only in the county wherein he resides or is employed or transacts his business in person, or at such other convenient place as is fixed by an order of court. A nonresident of the state may be required to attend only in the state and county wherein he is served with a subpoena, or within forty [40] miles from the place of service, or at such other convenient place as is fixed by an order of court. A non-resident plaintiff may be required to attend at his own expense an examination in the county of this state where the action is commenced or in a county fixed by the court.

(E) Subpoena for a hearing or trial. At the request of any party subpoenas for attendance at a hearing or trial shall be issued by the clerk of court of the county in which the action is pending when requested, or, in the case of a subpoena for the taking of a deposition, by the clerk of court of the county in which the action is so pending or in the county in which the deposition is being taken. An attorney admitted to practice law in this state, as an officer of the court, may also issue and sign such subpoenas on behalf of the court in which the action is pending or a court of the county in which the deposition is being taken, if the hearing, deposition or production pertains to an action pending in a court where the attorney has appeared for a party in that case. A subpoena may be served at any place within the state; and when permitted by the laws of the United States, this or another state or foreign country, the court upon proper application and cause shown may authorize the service of a subpoena outside the state in accordance with and as permitted by such law.

(F) Contempt. Failure by any person without adequate excuse to obey a subpoena served upon him may be deemed a contempt of the court from which the subpoena issued, or court of the county where the witness was required thereunder to appear or act. The attendance of all witnesses when duly subpoenaed, and to whom fees have been paid or tendered as required by law may be enforced by attachment.

(G) Tender of fees. Service of a subpoena upon a person named therein shall be made by delivering a copy thereof to such person who shall be required to attend outside his county of residence as provided in section (C), and by so tendering to him the fees for one [1] day's attendance and the mileage allowed by law. Such tender shall not be required to be made to a party who is subpoenaed or to an officer, employee, agent or representative of a party which is an organization, including the estate or any governmental organization, who is being examined upon any matter connected in any way with his employment or with duties to the organization.

(H) Proof of service of subpoena--Fees. When a subpoena is served by the sheriff or his deputy, his return shall be proof of service. When served by any other person the service must be shown by affidavit. No fees or costs for the service of a subpoena shall be collected or charged as costs except when service is made by the sheriff or his deputy.

Rule 46. Exceptions unnecessary

Formal exceptions to rulings or orders of the court are unnecessary; but for all purposes for which an exception has heretofore been necessary it is sufficient that a party, at the time the ruling or order of the court is made or sought, makes known to the court the action which he desires the court to take or his objection to the action of the court and his grounds therefor; and, if a party has no opportunity to object to a ruling or order at the time it is made, the absence of an objection does not thereafter prejudice him.

Rule 47. Jurors and peremptory challenges

(A) Number of jurors in civil cases. In all civil cases, the jury shall consist of six (6) members.

(B) Alternate Jurors. The Court may direct that no more than three (3) jurors in addition to the regular jury be called and impanelled to sit as alternate jurors. Alternate jurors in the order in which they are called shall replace jurors who, prior to the time the jury returns its verdict, become or are found to be unable or disqualified to perform their duties. Alternate jurors shall be drawn in the same manner, shall have the same qualifications, shall be subject to the same examination and challenges, shall take the same oath, and shall have the same functions, powers, facilities and privileges as the regular jurors. An alternate juror who does not replace a regular juror shall be discharged after the jury brings in its verdict. If alternate jurors are permitted to attend deliberations, they shall be instructed not to participate.

(C) Peremptory Challenges.

(1) Each side shall have three (3) peremptory challenges.

(2) In addition to the peremptory challenges under subsection (1), each side is entitled to:

(a) one (1) peremptory challenge if the court directs that one (1) or two alternate jurors are to be impanelled; or

(b) two (2) peremptory challenges if the court directs that three (3) alternate jurors are to be impanelled.

(3) The additional peremptory challenges under subsection (2) may be used only against alternate jurors and the peremptory challenges under subsection (1) may not be used against alternate jurors.

(D) Examination of jurors. The court shall permit the parties or their attorneys to conduct the examination of prospective jurors, and may conduct examination itself. The court's examination may include questions, if any, submitted in writing by any party or attorney. If the court conducts the examination, it shall permit the parties or their attorneys to supplement the examination by further inquiry. The court may impose an advance time limitation upon such examination by the parties or their attorneys. At the expiration of said limitation, the court shall liberally grant additional reasonable time upon a showing of good cause related to the nature of the case, the quantity of prospective jurors examined and juror vacancies remaining, and the manner and content of the inquiries and responses given by the prospective jurors. The court may prohibit the parties and their attorneys from examination which is repetitive, argumentative, or otherwise improper but shall permit reasonable inquir of the panel and individual prospective jurors.

Rule 48. Juries of less than six--Majority verdict

The parties may stipulate that the jury shall consist of any number less than six (6) at any time before the jury is selected or that a verdict or a finding of a stated majority of the jurors shall be taken as the verdict or finding of the jury at any time before the verdict has been announced.

Rule 49. Special verdicts and interrogatories

Special verdicts and interrogatories to the jury are abolished.

Rule 50. Judgment on the Evidence (Directed Verdict)

(A) Judgment on the Evidence--How Raised--Effect. Where all or some of the issues in a case tried before a jury or an advisory jury are not supported by sufficient evidence or a verdict thereon is clearly erroneous as contrary to the evidence because the evidence is insufficient to support it, the court shall withdraw such issues from the jury and enter judgment thereon or shall enter judgment thereon notwithstanding a verdict. A party may move for such judgment on the evidence.

(1) after another party carrying the burden of proof or of going forward with the evidence upon any one or more issues has completed presentation of his evidence thereon; or

(2) after all the parties have completed presentation of the evidence upon any one or more issues; or

(3) after all the evidence in the case has been presented and before judgment; or

(4) in a motion to correct errors; or

(5) may raise the issue upon appeal for the first time in criminal appeals but not in civil cases; or

(6) The trial court upon its own motion may enter such a judgment on the evidence at any time before final judgment, or before the filing of a notice of appeal, or, if a Motion to Correct Error is made, at any time before entering its order or ruling thereon. A party who moves for judgment on the evidence at the close of the evidence offered by an opponent may offer evidence in the event that the motion is not granted, without having reserved the right so to do and to the same extent as if the motion had not been made. A motion for a judgment on the evidence which is not granted or which is granted only as to a part of the issues is not a waiver of trial by jury even though all parties to the action have moved for judgment on the evidence. A motion for judgment on the evidence made at one stage of the proceedings is not a waiver of the right of the court or of any party to make such motion on the same or different issues or reasons at a later stage as permitted above, except that error of the court in denying the motion shall be deemed corrected by evidence thereafter offered or admitted.

(B) Jury trial subject to entry of judgment on the evidence. Every case tried by a jury is made subject to the right of the court, before or after the jury is discharged, to enter final judgment on the evidence, without directing a verdict thereon.

(C) New trial in lieu of judgment on the evidence. When a judgment on the evidence is sought before or after the jury is discharged, the court may grant a new trial as to part or all of the issues in lieu of a judgment on the evidence when entry of a judgment is impracticable or unfair to any of the parties or otherwise is improper, whether requested or not.

(D) Reasons for judgment on the evidence--Partial relief. A motion or request for judgment on the evidence shall state the reasons therefor, but it need not be accompanied by a peremptory instruction or prayer for particular relief. In appropriate cases the court, in whole or in part, may grant to some or all of the parties a judgment on the evidence or new trial in lieu thereof. Unless otherwise specified a motion or request for a judgment on the evidence is general, but the court shall grant such judgment or relief only as is proper.

(E) Motion for judgment notwithstanding verdict, motion in arrest of judgment, demurrer to the evidence and venire de novo abolished. The motion for judgment notwithstanding verdict, motion in arrest of judgment, demurrer to the evidence, and venire de novo are abolished.

Rule 51. Instructions to jury: Objections, requests: Submission in stages

(A) Preliminary Instructions. When the jury has been sworn the court shall instruct the jury in accordance with Jury Rule 20. Each party shall have reasonable opportunity to examine these preliminary instructions and state his specific objections thereto out of the presence of the jury and before any party has stated his case. (The court may of its own motion and, if requested by either party, shall reread to the jury all or any part of such preliminary instructions along with the other instructions given to the jury at the close of the case. A request to reread any preliminary instruction does not count against the ten [10] instructions provided in subsection (D) below.) The parties shall be given reasonable opportunity to submit requested instructions prior to the swearing of the jury, and object to instructions requested or proposed to be given.

(B) Final Instructions. The judge shall instruct the jury as to the law upon the issues presented by the evidence in accordance with Jury Rule 26.

(C) Objections and requested instructions before submission. At the close of the evidence and before argument each party may file written requests that the court instruct the jury on the law as set forth in the requests. The court shall inform counsel of its proposed action upon the requests prior to their arguments to the jury. No party may claim as error the giving of an instruction unless he objects thereto before the jury retires to consider its verdict, stating distinctly the matter to which he objects and the grounds of his objection. Opportunity shall be given to make the objection out of the hearing of the jury. The court shall note all instructions given, refused or tendered, and all written objections submitted thereto, shall be filed in open court and become a part of the record. Objections made orally shall be taken by the reporter and thereby shall become a part of the record.

(D) Limit upon requested instructions. Each party shall be entitled to tender no more than ten [10] requested instructions, including pattern instructions, to be given to the jury; however, the court in its discretion for good cause shown may fix a greater number. Each tendered instruction shall be confined to one [1] relevant legal principle. No party shall be entitled to predicate error upon the refusal of a trial court to give any tendered instruction in excess of the number fixed by this rule or the number fixed by the court order, whichever is greater.

(E) Indiana Pattern Jury Instructions (Criminal)/Indiana Model Jury Instructions (Civil). Any party requesting a trial court to give any instruction from the Indiana Pattern Jury Instructions (Criminal)/Indiana Model Jury Instructions (Civil), prepared under the sponsorship of the Indiana Judges Association, may make such request in writing without copying the instruction verbatim, by merely designating the number thereof in the publication.

Rule 52. Findings by the Court

(A) Effect. In the case of issues tried upon the facts without a jury or with an advisory jury, the court shall determine the facts and judgment shall be entered thereon pursuant to Rule 58. Upon its own motion, or the written request of any party filed with the court prior to the admission of evidence, the court in all actions tried upon the facts without a jury or with an advisory jury (except as provided in Rule 39[D]) shall find the facts specially and state its conclusions thereon. The court shall make special findings of fact without request

(1) in granting or refusing preliminary injunctions;

(2) in any review of actions by an administrative agency; and

(3) in any other case provided by these rules or by statute.

On appeal of claims tried by the court without a jury or with an advisory jury, at law or in equity, the court on appeal shall not set aside the findings or judgment unless clearly erroneous, and due regard shall be given to the opportunity of the trial court to judge the credibility of the witnesses. The findings of a master, and answers to questions or interrogatories submitted to the jury shall be considered as findings of the court to the extent that the court adopts them. If an opinion or memorandum of decision is filed, it will be sufficient if the findings of fact and conclusions appear therein. Findings of fact are unnecessary on decisions of motions under Rules 12 or 56 or any other motion except as provided in Rule 41(B) (dismissal) and 59(J) (motion to correct errors).

(B) Amendment of findings and judgment--causes therefor. Upon its own motion at any time before a motion to correct errors (Rule 59) is required to be made, or with or as part of a motion to correct errors by any party, the court, in the case of a claim tried without a jury or with an advisory jury, may open the judgment, if one has been entered, take additional testimony, amend or make new findings of fact and enter a new judgment or any combination thereof if:

(1) the judgment or findings are either against the weight of the evidence, or are not supported by or contrary to the evidence;

(2) special findings of fact required by this rule are lacking, incomplete, inadequate in form or content or do not cover the issues raised by the pleadings or evidence;

(3) special findings of fact required by this rule are inconsistent with each other; or

(4) the judgment is inconsistent with the special findings of fact required by this rule.

Failure of a party to move to modify the findings or judgment under this subdivision and failure to object to proposed findings or judgment or such findings or judgment which has been entered of record shall not constitute a waiver of the right to raise the question in or with a motion to correct errors, or on appeal.

(C) Proposed findings. In any case where special findings of facts and conclusions thereon are to be made the court shall allow and may require the attorneys of the parties to submit to the court a draft of findings of facts and conclusions thereon which they propose or suggest that the court make in such a case.

(D) Findings upon part of the issues. The court may make special findings of fact upon less than all the issues in a case when:

(1) special findings of fact are made but are not required under this rule; or

(2) findings are required because of the request of a party or parties who have demanded findings only upon such specified issues.

The court's failure to find upon a material issue upon which a finding of fact is required by this subdivision or this rule shall not be resolved by any presumption and may be challenged under subdivision (B) of this rule; but findings of fact with respect to issues upon which findings are not required shall be recognized as findings only upon the issues or matters covered thereby and the judgment or general finding, if any, shall control as to the other issues or matters which are not covered by such findings.

Rule 53. Masters

(A) Appointment and compensation. Each trial court with the concurrence of the Supreme Court may appoint a special master in a case pending therein. As used in these rules the word "master" includes without limitation an attorney, a referee, an auditor, an examiner, a commissioner, and an assessor. The compensation to be allowed to a master shall be allowed in the manner and amount paid to judges pro tem and such additional compensation as is fixed by the Supreme Court.

(B) Reference. A reference to a master shall be the exception and not the rule. In actions to be tried by a jury, a reference shall be made only when the issues are complicated; in actions to be tried without a jury, save in matters of account and of difficult computation of damages, a reference shall be made only upon a showing that some exceptional condition requires it. Reference shall be allowed when the parties agree prior to trial as provided by these rules or by statute.

(C) Powers. The order of reference to the master may specify or limit his powers and may direct him to report only upon particular issues or to do or perform particular acts or to receive and report evidence only and may fix the time and place for beginning and closing the hearings and for the filing of the master's report. Subject to the specifications and limitations stated in the order, the master has and shall exercise the power to regulate all proceedings in every hearing before him and to do all acts and take all measures necessary or proper for the efficient performance of his duties under the order. He may require the production before him of evidence upon all matters embraced in the reference, including the production of all books, papers, vouchers, documents, and writings applicable thereto. He may rule upon the admissibility of evidence unless otherwise directed by the order of reference and has the authority to put witnesses on oath and may himself examine them and may call the parties to the action and examine them upon oath. When a party so requests, the master shall make a record of the evidence offered and excluded in the same manner and subject to the same limitations as provided in Rule 43(C) for a court sitting without a jury.

(D) Proceedings.

(1) Meetings. When a reference is made, the clerk shall forthwith furnish the master with a copy of the order of reference. Upon receipt thereof unless the order of reference otherwise provides, the master shall forthwith set a time and place for the first meeting of the parties or their attorneys to be held within twenty [20] days after the date of the order of reference and shall notify the parties or their attorneys. It is the duty of the master to proceed with all reasonable diligence. Either party, on notice to the parties and master, may apply to the court for an order requiring the master to speed the proceedings and to make his report. If a party fails to appear at the time and place appointed, the master may proceed ex parte or, in his discretion, adjourn the proceedings to a future day, giving notice to the absent party of the adjournment.

(2) Witnesses. The parties may procure the attendance of witnesses before the master by the issuance and service of subpoenas as provided in Rule 45. If without adequate excuse a witness fails to appear or give evidence, he may be punished as for a contempt and be subjected to the consequences, penalties, and remedies provided in Rules 37 and 45.

(3) Statement of accounts. When matters of accounting are in issue before the master, he may prescribe the form in which the amounts shall be submitted and in any proper case may require or receive in evidence a statement by a certified public accountant who is called as a witness. Upon objection of a party to any of the

items thus submitted or upon a showing that the form of statement is insufficient, the master may require a different form of statement to be furnished, or the accounts or specific items thereof to be provided by oral examination of the accounting parties or upon written interrogatories or in such other manner as he directs.

(E) Report.

(1) Contents and filing. The master shall prepare a report upon the matters submitted to him by the order of reference and, if required by request of any party or the court prior to hearing or the taking of evidence by him to make findings of fact, he shall set them forth in the report. He shall file the report with the clerk of the court and in an action to be tried without a jury, unless otherwise directed by the order of reference, shall file with it a transcript of the proceedings and of the evidence and the original exhibits. The clerk shall forthwith mail to all parties notice of the filing.

(2) In nonjury actions. In an action to be tried without a jury the court shall accept the master's decision or his findings of fact unless clearly erroneous. Within ten [10] days after being served with notice of the filing of the report any party may serve written objections thereto upon the other parties. Application to the court for action upon the report and upon objections thereto shall be by motion and upon notice as prescribed in Rules 5 and 6. The court after hearing may adopt the report or may reject it in whole or in part or may receive further evidence or may re-commit it with instructions.

(3) In jury actions. In an action to be tried by a jury the master shall not be directed to report the evidence. His findings upon the issues submitted to him are admissible as evidence of the matters found and may be read to the jury, subject to the ruling of the court upon any objections in point of law which may be made to the report.

(4) Stipulation as to findings. The effect of a master's report is the same whether or not the parties have consented to the reference; but, when the parties stipulate that a master's findings of fact shall be final, only questions of law arising upon the report shall thereafter be considered.

(5) Draft report. Before filing his report a master may submit a draft thereof to counsel for all parties for the purpose of receiving their suggestions.

(F) Particular laws not affected. Nothing in this rule shall affect laws providing for the appointment and duties of probate commissioners; and nothing shall prevent any probate or other similar court from appointing a master under this rule.

Rule 53.1. Failure to rule on motion

(A) Time limitation for ruling. In the event a court fails for thirty (30) days to set a motion for hearing or fails to rule on a motion within thirty (30) days after it was heard or thirty (30) days after it was filed, if no hearing is required, upon application by an interested party, the submission of the cause may be withdrawn from the trial judge and transferred to the Supreme Court for the appointment of a special judge.

(B) Exceptions. The time limitation for ruling on a motion established under Section (A) of this rule shall exclude any period after which the case is referred to alternative dispute resolution and until a report on the alternative dispute resolution is submitted to the court. The time limitation for ruling on a motion established under Section (A) of this rule shall not apply where:

(1) The Court, within thirty (30) days after filing, orders that a motion be considered during the trial on the merits of the cause; or

(2) The parties who have appeared or their counsel stipulate or agree on record that the time limitation for ruling on a motion shall not apply; or

(3) The time limitation for ruling has been extended by the Supreme Court as provided by Section (D) of this rule; or

(4) The ruling in question involves a repetitive motion, a motion to reconsider, a motion to correct error, a petition for post-conviction relief, or a ministerial post-judgment act.

(C) Time of ruling. For the purposes of Section (A) of this rule, a court is deemed to have set a motion for hearing on the date the setting is noted in the Chronological Case Summary, and to have ruled on the date the ruling is noted in the Chronological Case Summary.

(D) Extension of time for ruling. A judge may apply to the Supreme Court of Indiana to extend the time limitation set forth under Trial Rule 53.1, 53.2, or 53.3. The application must be filed prior to the filing of a praecipe with the Clerk under Trial Rules 53.1, 53.2, or 53.3, must be verified, must be served on the Clerk and all parties of record, and must set forth the following information:

(1) The nature of the matter under submission;

(2) The circumstances warranting the delay; and

(3) The additional time requested.

The withdrawal of submission under Trial Rule 53.1 or 53.2 or denial of a motion to correct error under Trial Rule 53.3 may not take effect during the pendency of the application for an extension of time to rule. However, the time limitation expires while the application is pending before the Supreme Court, the jurisdiction of the trial judge shall be suspended at that point pending the action of the Supreme Court.

(E) Procedure for withdrawing submission. Upon the filing by an interested party of a praecipe specifically designating the motion or decision delayed, the Clerk of the court shall enter the date and time of the filing on the praecipe, record the filing in the Chronological Case Summary under the cause, which entry shall also include the date and time of the filing of the praecipe, and promptly forward the praecipe and a copy of the Chronological Case Summary to the Chief Administrative Officer (CAO)of the Indiana Office of Judicial Administration (IOJA). The CAO shall determine whether or not a ruling has been delayed beyond the time limitation set forth under Trial Rule 53.1 or 53.2.

(1) If the CAO determines that the ruling or decision has not been delayed, the CAO shall provide notice of th determination in writing to the Clerk of the court where the case is pending and the submission of the cause shall not be withdrawn. The Clerk of the court where the case in pending shall notify, in writing, the judge and all parties of record in the proceeding and record the determination in the Chronological Case Summary under the cause.

(2) If the CAO determines that a ruling or decision has been delayed beyond the time limitation set forth und Trial Rule 53.1 or 53.2, the CAO shall give written notice of the determination to the judge, the Clerk of th trial court, and the Clerk of the Supreme Court of Indiana that the submission of the case has been withdrawn from the judge. The withdrawal is effective as of the time of the filing of the praecipe. The Cler of the trial court shall record this determination in the Chronological Case Summary under the cause and provide notice to all parties in the case. The CAO shall submit the case to the Supreme Court of Indiana fo appointment of a special judge or such other action deemed appropriate by the Supreme Court.

(F) Report to Supreme Court. When a special judge is appointed under Trial Rule 53.1 or 53.2, the judge from whom submission was withdrawn shall, within ten (10) days from receipt of the order appointing a special judge, file a written report in the Supreme Court under the cause appointing the special judge. This report shal fully state the nature of the matters held in excess of the time limitations. Additionally, the report may relate ar other facts or circumstances which the judge deems pertinent.

(G) Permanent record. The Supreme Court shall maintain a permanent record of special judge appointments under Trial Rules 53.1 and 53.2.

Rule 53.2. Time for holding issue under advisement; delay of entering a judgment

(A) Time limitation for holding matter under advisement. Whenever a cause (including for this purpose a petition for post conviction relief) has been tried to the court and taken under advisement by the judge, and the judge fails to determine any issue of law or fact within ninety (90) days, the submission of all the pending issue and the cause may be withdrawn from the trial judge and transferred to the Supreme Court for the appointmen of a special judge.

(B) Exceptions. The time limitation for holding an issue under advisement established under Section (A) of this rule shall not apply where:

(1) The parties who have appeared or their counsel stipulate or agree on record that the time limitation for decision set forth in this rule shall not apply; or

(2) The time limitation for decision has been extended by the Supreme Court pursuant to Trial Rule 53.1(D).

(C) Time of decision. For the purpose of Section (A) of this rule, a court is deemed to have decided on the date the decision is noted in the Chronological Case Summary.

(D) Extension of time for decision. The procedure for extending the time limitation for decision shall be as set forth in Trial Rule 53.1(D).

(E) Procedure for withdrawing submission. The procedure for withdrawing submission and processing the appointment of a special judge shall be as set forth in Trial Rule 53.1(E).

(F) Report to Supreme Court. Whenever a special judge is appointed pursuant to this rule, the judge from whom submission has been withdrawn shall file a report with the Supreme Court as provided for in Trial Rule 53.1(F).

Rule 53.3. Motion to correct error: time limitation for ruling

(A) Time limitation for ruling on motion to correct error. In the event a court fails for forty-five (45) days to set a Motion to Correct Error for hearing, or fails to rule on a Motion to Correct Error within thirty (30) days after it was heard or forty-five (45) days after it was filed, if no hearing is required, the pending Motion to Correct Error shall be deemed denied. Any appeal shall be initiated by filing the notice of appeal under Appellate Rule 9(A) within thirty (30) days after the Motion to Correct Error is deemed denied.

(B) Exceptions. The time limitation for ruling on a motion to correct error established under Section (A) of this rule shall not apply where:

(1) The party has failed to serve the judge personally; or

(2) The parties who have appeared or their counsel stipulate or agree on record that the time limitation for ruling set forth under Section (A) shall not apply; or

(3) The time limitation for ruling has been extended by Section (D) of this rule.

(C) Time of ruling. For the purposes of Section (A) of this rule, a court is deemed to have set a motion for hearing on the date the setting is noted in the Chronological Case Summary, and to have ruled on the date the ruling is noted in the Chronological Case Summary.

(D) Extension of time for ruling. The Judge before whom a Motion to Correct Error is pending may extend the time limitation for ruling for a period of no more than thirty (30) days by filing an entry in the cause advising all parties of the extension. Such entry must be in writing, must be noted in the Chronological Case Summary before the expiration of the initial time period for ruling set forth under Section (A), and must be served on all parties. Additional extension of time may be granted only upon application to the Supreme Court as set forth in Trial Rule 53.1(D).

Rule 53.4. Repetitive motions and motions to reconsider; time for holding under advisement; automatic denial

(A) Repetitive motions and motions to reconsider ruling on a motion. No hearing shall be required upon a repetitive motion or upon motions to reconsider orders or rulings upon a motion. Such a motion by any party or the court or such action to reconsider by the court shall not delay the trial or any proceedings in the case, or extend the time for any further required or permitted action, motion, or proceedings under these rules.

(B) Effect of court's delay in ruling upon repetitive motion or motion to reconsider ruling on a motion. Unless such a motion is ruled upon within five (5) days it shall be deemed denied, and entry of service of notice of such denial shall not be required. This Rule 53.4 does not apply to an original motion for judgment on the evidence under Rule 50 after the jury is discharged, to amend or make additional findings of fact under Rule 52(B), an original motion to correct errors under Rule 59, or for correction of relief from judgments under Rule 60 or to the original motions to the extent expressly permitted or expressly designated as extending time under these rules.

Rule 53.5. Continuances

Upon motion, trial may be postponed or continued in the discretion of the court, and shall be allowed upon a showing of good cause established by affidavit or other evidence. The court may award such costs as will reimburse the other parties for their actual expenses incurred from the delay. A motion to postpone the trial on account of the absence of evidence can be made only upon affidavit, showing the materiality of the evidence expected to be obtained, and that due diligence has been used to obtain it; and where the evidence may be; and if it is for an absent witness, the affidavit must show the name and residence of the witness, if known, and the probability of procuring the testimony within a reasonable time, and that his absence has not been procured by the act or connivance of the party, nor by others at his request, nor with his knowledge and consent, and what facts he believes to be true, and that he is unable to prove such facts by any other witness whose testimony can be as readily procured. If, thereupon, the adverse party will consent that, on the trial, the facts shall be taken as true if the absent evidence is written or documentary, and, in case of a witness, that he will testify to said facts as true, the trial shall not be postponed for that cause, and in such case, the party against whom such evidence is used, shall have the right to impeach such absent witness, as in the case where the witness is present, or his deposition is used.

Rule 54. Judgment; Costs

(A) Definition-Form. "Judgment", as used in these rules, includes a decree and any order from which an appeal lies. A judgment shall contain all matters required by Rule 58 but need not contain a recital of pleadings, the report of a master, or the record of prior proceedings.

(B) Judgment upon multiple claims or involving multiple parties. When more than one [1] claim for relie is presented in an action, whether as a claim, counterclaim, cross-claim, or third-party claim, or when multiple parties are involved, the court may direct the entry of a final judgment as to one or more but fewer than all of the claims or parties only upon an express determination that there is no just reason for delay and upon an express direction for the entry of judgment. In the absence of such determination and direction, any order or other form of decision, however designated, which adjudicates fewer than all the claims or the rights and liabilities of fewer than all the parties shall not terminate the action as to any of the claims or parties, and the order or other form of decision is subject to revision at any time before the entry of judgment adjudicating all the claims and the rights and liabilities of all the parties. A judgment as to one or more but fewer than all of the claims or parties is final when the court in writing expressly determines that there is no just reason for delay, and in writing expressly directs entry of judgment, and an appeal may be taken upon this or other issues resolved by the judgment; but in other cases a judgment, decision or order as to less than all the claims and parties is not final.

(C) Demand for judgment. A judgment by default shall not be different in kind from or exceed in amount that prayed for in the demand for judgment. Except as to a party against whom a judgment is entered by default, every final judgment shall grant the relief to which the party in whose favor it is rendered is entitled, even if the party has not demanded such relief in his pleadings.

(D) Costs. Except when express provision therefor is made either in a statute or in these rules, costs shall be allowed as of course to the prevailing party unless the court otherwise directs in accordance with any provision of law; but costs against any governmental organization, its officers, and agencies shall be imposed only to the extent permitted by law. Costs may be computed and taxed by the clerk on one [1] day's notice. On motion served within five [5] days thereafter, the action of the clerk may be reviewed by the court.

(E) Judgments severable. Unless otherwise specified therein, judgments against two [2] or more persons or upon two [2] or more claims shall be deemed joint and several for purposes of:

(1) permitting enforcement proceedings jointly or separately against different parties or jointly or separately against their property; or

(2) permitting one or more parties to challenge the judgment (by appeal, motion and the like) as against one o more parties as to one or more claims or parts of claims.

Nothing herein is intended to dispense with notice requirements, or provisions requiring or permitting parties to join or participate in the same appeal.

Rule 55. Default

(A) Entry. When a party against whom a judgment for affirmative relief is sought has failed to plead or otherwise comply with these rules and that fact is made to appear by affidavit or otherwise, the party may be defaulted by the court.

(B) Default judgment. In all cases the party entitled to a judgment by default shall apply to the court therefor; but no judgment by default shall be entered against a person (1) known to be an infant or incompetent unless represented in the action by a general guardian, committee, conservator, or other such representative who has appeared therein; or (2) entitled to the protections against default judgments provided by the Servicemembers Civil Relief Act, as amended (the "Act"), 50 U.S.C. appx. § 521, unless the requirements of the Act have been complied with. See Ind. Small Claims Rule 10(B)(3). If the party against whom judgment by default is sought has appeared in the action, he (or, if appearing by a representative, his representative) shall be served with written notice of the application for judgment at least three [3] days prior to the hearing on such application. If, in order to enable the court to enter judgment or to carry it into effect, it is necessary to take an account or to determine the amount of damages or to establish the truth of any averment by evidence or to make an investigation of any other matter, the court may conduct such hearing or order such references as it deems necessary and proper and shall accord a right of trial by jury to the parties when and as required.

(C) Setting aside default. A judgment by default which has been entered may be set aside by the court for the grounds and in accordance with the provisions of Rule 60(B).

(D) Plaintiff, counterclaimants, cross-claimants. The provisions of this rule apply whether the party entitled to the judgment by default is a plaintiff, a third-party plaintiff, or a party who has pleaded a cross-claim or counterclaim. In all cases a judgment by default is subject to the limitations of Rule 54(C).

(E) Judgment against governmental organizations. A judgment by default may be entered against a governmental organization.

ule 56. Summary judgment

(A) For claimant. A party seeking to recover upon a claim, counterclaim, or cross-claim or to obtain a declaratory judgment may, at any time after the expiration of twenty [20] days from the commencement of the action or after service of a motion for summary judgment by the adverse party, move with or without supporting affidavits for a summary judgment in his favor upon all or any part thereof.

(B) For defending party--When motion not required. A party against whom a claim, counterclaim, or cross-claim is asserted or a declaratory judgment is sought may, at any time, move with or without supporting affidavits for a summary judgment in his favor as to all or any part thereof. When any party has moved for summary judgment, the court may grant summary judgment for any other party upon the issues raised by the motion although no motion for summary judgment is filed by such party.

(C) Motion and proceedings thereon. The motion and any supporting affidavits shall be served in accordance with the provisions of Rule 5. An adverse party shall have thirty (30) days after service of the motion to serve a response and any opposing affidavits. The court may conduct a hearing on the motion. However, upon motion of any party made no later than ten (10) days after the response was filed or was due, the court shall conduct a hearing on the motion which shall be held not less than ten (10) days after the time for filing the response. At the time of filing the motion or response, a party shall designate to the court all parts of pleadings, depositions, answers to interrogatories, admissions, matters of judicial notice, and any other matters on which it relies for purposes of the motion. A party opposing the motion shall also designate to the court each material issue of fact which that party asserts precludes entry of summary judgment and the evidence relevant thereto. The judgment sought shall be rendered forthwith if the designated evidentiary matter shows that there is no genuine issue as to any material fact and that the moving party is entitled to a judgment as a matter of law. A summary judgment may be rendered upon less than all the issues or claims, including without limitation the issue of liability or damages alone although there is a genuine issue as to damages or liability as the case may be. A summary judgment upon less than all the issues involved in a claim or with respect to less than all the claims or parties shall be interlocutory unless the court in writing expressly determines that there is no just reason for delay and in writing expressly directs entry of judgment as to less than all the issues, claims or parties. The court shall designate the issues or claims upon which it finds no genuine issue as to any material facts. Summary judgment shall not be granted as of course because the opposing party fails to offer opposing affidavits or evidence, but the court shall make its determination from the evidentiary matter designated to the court.

(D) Case not fully adjudicated on motion. If on motion under this rule judgment is not rendered upon the whole case or for all the relief asked and a trial is necessary, the court at the hearing of the motion, by examining the pleadings and the evidence before it and by interrogating counsel, shall if practicable ascertain what material facts exist without substantial controversy and what material facts are actually and in good faith controverted. It shall thereupon make an order specifying the facts that appear without substantial controversy, including the extent to which the amount of damages or other relief is not in controversy, and directing such further proceedings in the action as are just. Upon the trial of the action the facts so specified shall be deemed established, and the trial shall be conducted accordingly.

(E) Form of affidavits--Further testimony--Defense required. Supporting and opposing affidavits shall be made on personal knowledge, shall set forth such facts as would be admissible in evidence, and shall show affirmatively that the affiant is competent to testify to the matters stated therein. Sworn or certified copies not previously self-authenticated of all papers or parts thereof referred to in an affidavit shall be attached thereto or served therewith. The court may permit affidavits to be supplemented or opposed by depositions, answers to interrogatories, or further affidavits. When a motion for summary judgment is made and supported as provided in this rule, an adverse party may not rest upon the mere allegations or denials of his pleading, but his response, by affidavits or as otherwise provided in this rule, must set forth specific facts showing that there is a genuine issue for trial. If he does not so respond, summary judgment, if appropriate, shall be entered against him. Denial of summary judgment may be challenged by a motion to correct errors after a final judgment or order is entered.

(F) When affidavits are unavailable. Should it appear from the affidavits of a party opposing the motion that he cannot for reasons stated present by affidavit facts essential to justify his opposition, the court may refuse the application for judgment or may order a continuance to permit affidavits to be obtained or depositions to be taken or discovery to be had or may make such other order as is just.

(G) Affidavits made in bad faith. Should it appear to the satisfaction of the court at any time that any of the affidavits presented pursuant to this rule are presented in bad faith or solely for the purpose of delay, the court shall forthwith order the party employing them to pay to the other party the amount of the reasonable expenses which the filing of the affidavits caused him to incur, including reasonable attorney's fees, and any offending party or attorney may be adjudged guilty of contempt.

(H) **Appeal-Reversal.** No judgment rendered on the motion shall be reversed on the ground that there is a genuine issue of material fact unless the material fact and the evidence relevant thereto shall have been specifically designated to the trial court.

(I) **Alteration of Time.** For cause found, the Court may alter any time limit set forth in this rule upon motion made within the applicable time limit.

Rule 57. Declaratory judgments

The procedure for obtaining a declaratory judgment shall be in accordance with these rules, and the right to trial by jury may be demanded under the circumstances and in the manner provided in Rules 38 and 39. The existence of another adequate remedy does not preclude a judgment for declaratory relief in cases where it is appropriate. Declaratory relief shall be allowed even though a property right is not involved. Affirmative relief shall be allowed under such remedy when the right thereto is established. The court may order a speedy hearing of an action for a declaratory judgment and may advance it on the calendar.

Rule 58. Entry and content of judgment

(A) **Entry of judgment.** Subject to the provisions of Rule 54(B), upon a verdict of a jury, or upon a decision of the court, the court shall promptly prepare and sign the judgment, and the clerk shall thereupon enter the judgment in the Record of Judgments and Orders and note the entry of the judgment in the Chronological Case Summary and Judgment Docket. A judgment shall be set forth on a separate document, except that a judgment may appear upon the same document upon which appears the court's findings, conclusions, or opinion upon the issues. The entry of the judgment shall not be delayed for the taxing of costs. Attorneys may submit suggested forms of judgment to the court, and upon request of the court, shall assist the court in the preparation of a judgment, but the judgment shall not be delayed to await the resolution of issues by agreement of counsel. The judge failing promptly to cause the judgment to be prepared, signed and entered as provided herein may be compelled to do so by mandate.

(B) **Content of judgment.** Except in small claims cases, a judgment shall contain the following elements:

(1) A statement of the submission indicating whether the submission was to a jury or to the Court; whether the submission was upon default, motion, cross-claim, counterclaim or third-party complaint; and if the submission was to less than all issues or parties, such other matters as may be necessary to clearly state what issue is resolved or what party is bound by the judgment.

(2) A statement of the appearances at the submission indicating whether the parties appeared in person, by counsel, or both; whether there was a failure to appear after notice; and whether the submission was conducted by telephone conference.

(3) At the court's discretion and in such detail as it may deem appropriate, a statement of the court's jurisdiction over the parties and action and of the issues considered in sufficient particularity to enable any party affected by the judgment to raise in another action the defenses of merger, bar or claim or issue preclusion.

(4) A statement in imperative form which clearly and concisely sets forth the relief granted, any alteration of status, any right declared, or any act to be done or not done.

(5) The date of the judgment and the signature of the judge.

(C) **Court Records Excluded from Public Access and Confidential Pursuant to Administrative Rule 9(G).** Every court that issues a judgment or order containing Court Records excluded from Public Access pursuant to Administrative Rule 9(G) shall comply with the provisions of Administrative Rule 9(G)(5).

(D) **Satisfaction/Release of Judgment.** Upon payment in full of a judgment, including accrued interest and court costs, the judgment creditor shall file a satisfaction/release of judgment and the Clerk shall note the satisfaction/release of the judgment on the CCS and on the judgment docket.

Based upon a review of the Clerk's payment records, the Clerk may, or at the verified request of the judgment debtor shall, issue a Notice to the judgment creditor that a judgment, including accrued interest and court costs, has been paid in full and that the judgment should be satisfied/released. The Notice shall be sent to the judgment creditor and debtor at the address shown on the Chronological Case Summary. The Clerk shall note the issuance of the Notice on the Chronological Case Summary. If the judgment creditor does not agree that the judgment should be satisfied/released, the judgment creditor shall, within 30 days of the date of the issuance of the Notice, file a verified objection. If the judgment creditor does not file an objection or a satisfaction/release of judgment, the judgment shall be deemed satisfied/released and the Clerk shall note the satisfaction/release of the judgment on the Chronological Case Summary and on the Judgment Docket.

Rule 59. Motion to correct error

(A) Motion to correct error--When mandatory. A Motion to Correct Error is not a prerequisite for appeal, except when a party seeks to address:

(1) Newly discovered material evidence, including alleged jury misconduct, capable of production within thirty (30) days of final judgment which, with reasonable diligence, could not have been discovered and produced at trial; or

(2) A claim that a jury verdict is excessive or inadequate.

All other issues and grounds for appeal appropriately preserved during trial may be initially addressed in the appellate brief.

(B) Filing of motion. The motion to correct error, if any, may be made by the trial court, or by any party.

(C) Time for filing: Service on judge. The motion to correct error, if any, shall be filed not later than thirty (30) days after the entry of a final judgment is noted in the Chronological Case Summary. A copy of the motion to correct error shall be served, when filed, upon the judge before whom the case is pending pursuant to Trial Rule 5. The time at which the court is deemed to have ruled on the motion is set forth in T.R. 53.3.

(D) Errors raised by motion to correct error, and content of motion.

Where used, a motion to correct error need only address those errors found in Trial Rule 59(A)(1) and (2).

Any error raised however shall be stated in specific rather than general terms and shall be accompanied by a statement of facts and grounds upon which the error is based. The error claimed is not required to be stated under, or in the language of the bases for the motion allowed by this rule, by statute, or by other law.

(E) Statement in opposition to motion to correct error. Following the filing of a motion to correct error, a party who opposes the motion may file a statement in opposition to the motion to correct error not later than fifteen [15] days after service of the motion. The statement in opposition may assert grounds which show that the final judgment or appealable final order should remain unchanged, or the statement in opposition may present other grounds which show that the party filing the statement in opposition is entitled to other relief.

(F) Motion to correct error granted. Any modification or setting aside of a final judgment or an appealable final order following the filing of a Motion to Correct Error shall be an appealable final judgment or order.

(G) Cross errors. If a motion to correct error is denied, the party who prevailed on that motion may, in the appellate brief and without having filed a statement in opposition to the motion to correct error in the trial court, defend against the motion to correct error on any ground and may first assert grounds for relief therein, including grounds falling within sections (A)(1) and (2) of this rule. In addition, if a Notice of Appeal rather than a motion to correct error is filed by a party, the opposing party may raise any grounds as cross-errors and also may raise any reasons to affirm the judgment directly in the appellate brief, including those grounds for which a motion to correct error is required when directly appealing a judgment under Sections (A)(1) and (2) of this rule.

(H) Motion to correct error based on evidence outside the record.

(1) When a motion to correct error is based upon evidence outside the record, the motion shall be supported by affidavits showing the truth of the grounds set out in the motion and the affidavits shall be served with the motion.

(2) If a party opposes a motion to correct error made under this subdivision, that party has fifteen [15] days after service of the moving party's affidavits and motion, in which to file opposing affidavits.

(3) If a party opposes a motion to correct error made under this subdivision, that party has fifteen [15] days after service of the moving party's affidavits and motion, in which to file its own motion to correct errors under this subdivision, and in which to assert relevant matters which relate to the kind of relief sought by the party first moving to correct error under this subdivision.

(4) No reply affidavits, motions, or other papers from the party first moving to correct errors are contemplated under this subdivision.

(I) Costs in the event a new trial is ordered. The trial court, in granting a new trial, may place costs upon the party who applied for the new trial, or a portion of the costs, or it may place costs abiding the event of the suit, or it may place all costs or a portion of the costs on either or all parties as justice and equity in the case may require after the trial court has taken into consideration the causes which made the new trial necessary.

(J) Relief granted on motion to correct error. The court, if it determines that prejudicial or harmful error has been committed, shall take such action as will cure the error, including without limitation the following with respect to all or some of the parties and all or some of the errors:

(1) Grant a new trial;

(2) Enter final judgment;

(3) Alter, amend, modify or correct judgment;

(4) Amend or correct the findings or judgment as provided in Rule 52(B);

(5) In the case of excessive or inadequate damages, enter final judgment on the evidence for the amount of the proper damages, grant a new trial, or grant a new trial subject to additur or remittitur;

(6) Grant any other appropriate relief, or make relief subject to condition; or

(7) In reviewing the evidence, the court shall grant a new trial if it determines that the verdict of a non-advisory jury is against the weight of the evidence; and shall enter judgment, subject to the provisions herein, if the court determines that the verdict of a non-advisory jury is clearly erroneous as contrary to or not supported by the evidence, or if the court determines that the findings and judgment upon issues tried without a jury or with an advisory jury are against the weight of the evidence.

In its order correcting error the court shall direct final judgment to be entered or shall correct the error without a new trial unless such relief is shown to be impracticable or unfair to any of the parties or is otherwise improper; and if a new trial is required it shall be limited only to those parties and issues affected by the error unless such relief is shown to be impracticable or unfair. If corrective relief is granted, the court shall specify the general reasons therefor. When a new trial is granted because the verdict, findings or judgment do not accord with the evidence, the court shall make special findings of fact upon each material issue or element of the claim or defense upon which a new trial is granted. Such finding shall indicate whether the decision is against the weight of the evidence or whether it is clearly erroneous as contrary to or not supported by the evidence; if the decision is found to be against the weight of the evidence, the findings shall relate the supporting and opposing evidence to each issue upon which a new trial is granted; if the decision is found to be clearly erroneous as contrary to or not supported by the evidence, the findings shall show why judgment was not entered upon the evidence.

(K) Orders regarding services, programs, or placement of children alleged to be delinquents or alleged to be in need of services. No motion to correct error is allowed concerning orders or decrees issued pursuant to Indiana Code sections 31-34-4-7(e), 31-34-19-6.1(e), 31-37-5-8(f), or 31-37-18-9(b). Appeals of such orders and decrees shall proceed as prescribed by Indiana Appellate Rule 14.1.

Rule 60. Relief from judgment or order

(A) Clerical mistakes. Of its own initiative or on the motion of any party and after such notice, if any, as the court orders, clerical mistakes in judgments, orders or other parts of the record and errors therein arising from oversight or omission may be corrected by the trial court at any time before the Notice of Completion of Clerk's Record is filed under Appellate Rule 8. After filing of the Notice of Completion of Clerk's Record and during an appeal, such mistakes may be so corrected with leave of the court on appeal.

(B) Mistake--Excusable neglect--Newly discovered evidence--Fraud, etc. On motion and upon such terms as are just the court may relieve a party or his legal representative from a judgment, including a judgment by default, for the following reasons:

(1) mistake, surprise, or excusable neglect;

(2) any ground for a motion to correct error, including without limitation newly discovered evidence, which by due diligence could not have been discovered in time to move for a motion to correct errors under Rule 59;

(3) fraud (whether heretofore denominated intrinsic or extrinsic), misrepresentation, or other misconduct of an adverse party;

(4) entry of default or judgment by default was entered against such party who was served only by publication and who was without actual knowledge of the action and judgment, order or proceedings;

(5) except in the case of a divorce decree, the record fails to show that such party was represented by a guardian or other representative, and if the motion asserts and such party proves that

(a) at the time of the action he was an infant or incompetent person, and

(b) he was not in fact represented by a guardian or other representative, and

(c) the person against whom the judgment, order or proceeding is being avoided procured the judgment with notice of such infancy or incompetency, and, as against a successor of such person, that such successor acquired his rights therein with notice that the judgment was procured against an infant or incompetent, and

(d) no appeal or other remedies allowed under this subdivision have been taken or made by or on behalf of the infant or incompetent person, and

(e) the motion was made within ninety [90] days after the disability was removed or a guardian was appointed over his estate, and

(f) the motion alleges a valid defense or claim;

(6) the judgment is void;

(7) the judgment has been satisfied, released, or discharged, or a prior judgment upon which it is based has been reversed or otherwise vacated, or it is no longer equitable that the judgment should have prospective application; or

(8) any reason justifying relief from the operation of the judgment, other than those reasons set forth in sub-paragraphs (1), (2), (3), and (4).

The motion shall be filed within a reasonable time for reasons (5), (6), (7), and (8), and not more than one year after the judgment, order or proceeding was entered or taken for reasons (1), (2), (3), and (4). A movant filing a motion for reasons (1), (2), (3), (4), and (8) must allege a meritorious claim or defense. A motion under this subdivision (B) does not affect the finality of a judgment or suspend its operation. This rule does not limit the power of a court to entertain an independent action to relieve a party from a judgment, order or proceeding or for fraud upon the court. Writs of coram nobis, coram vobis, audita querela, and bills of review and bills in the nature of a bill of review, are abolished, and the procedure for obtaining any relief from a judgment shall be by motion as prescribed in these rules or by an independent action.

(C) Appeal--Change of venue. A ruling or order of the court denying or granting relief, in whole or in part, by motion under subdivision (B) of this rule shall be deemed a final judgment, and an appeal may be taken therefrom as in the case of a judgment. No change of venue in such cases shall be taken from the judge or county except for cause shown by affidavit.

(D) Hearing and relief granted. In passing upon a motion allowed by subdivision (B) of this rule the court shall hear any pertinent evidence, allow new parties to be served with summons, allow discovery, grant relief as provided under Rule 59 or otherwise as permitted by subdivision (B) of this rule.

(E) Infants, incompetents, and governmental organizations. Except as otherwise provided herein, this rule shall apply to infants, incompetents, and governmental organizations. The time for seeking relief against a judgment, order or proceeding allowed or recognized under subdivision (B) of this rule or any other statute shall not be tolled or extended as to such persons.

Rule 60.5. Mandate of funds

(A) Scope of mandate. Courts shall limit their requests for funds to those which are reasonably necessary for the operation of the court or court-related functions. Mandate will not lie for extravagant, arbitrary or unwarranted expenditures nor for personal expenditures (e.g., personal telephone bills, bar association memberships, disciplinary fees). Prior to issuing the order, the court shall meet with the mandated party to demonstrate the need for said funds. At any time in the process, the dispute may be submitted to mediation by agreement of the parties or by order of the Supreme Court or the special judge.

(B) Procedure. Whenever a court, except the Supreme Court or the Court of Appeals, desires to order either a municipality, a political subdivision of the state, or an officer of either to appropriate or to pay unappropriated funds for the operation of the court or court-related functions, such court shall issue and cause to be served upon such municipality, political subdivision or officer an order to show cause why such appropriation or payment should not be made. Such order to show cause shall be captioned "Order for Mandate of Funds". The matter shall be set for trial on the merits of such order to show cause unless the legislative body, the chief executive officer or the affected officer files a waiver in writing of such a trial and agrees to make such appropriation or payment. The trial shall be without a jury, before a special judge of the court that made the order. There shall be no change of venue from the county or from the special judge appointed by the Supreme Court. The court shall promptly notify the Supreme Court of the entry of such order to show cause and the Supreme Court shall then appoint as special judge an attorney who is not a current or former regular judge and who does not reside nor regularly practice law in the county issuing the Order of Mandate of Funds or in any county contiguous thereto. If the appointed judge fails to qualify within seven [7] days after he has received notice of his appointment, the Supreme Court shall follow the same procedure until an appointed judge does properly qualify. Unless expressly waived by the respondent in writing within thirty (30) days after the entering of the trial judge's decree, a decree or order mandating the payment of funds for the operation of the court or court-related functions shall be automatically reviewed by the Supreme Court. Promptly on expiration of such thirty (30) day period, the trial judge shall certify such decree together with either a stipulation of facts or an electronic transcription of the evidence to the Supreme Court. No motion to correct error nor notice of appeal shall be filed. No mandate order for appropriation or payment of funds made by any court other than the Supreme Court or Court of Appeals shall direct that attorney fees be paid at a rate greater than the reasonable and customary hourly rate for an attorney in the county. No mandate order shall be effective unless it is entered after trial as herein provided and until the order has been reviewed by the Supreme Court or such review is expressly waived as herein provided.

Rule 61. Harmless error

No error in either the admission or the exclusion of evidence and no error or defect in any ruling or order in anything done or omitted by the court or by any of the parties is ground for granting relief under a motion to correct errors or for setting aside a verdict or for vacating, modifying or otherwise disturbing a judgment or order or for reversal on appeal, unless refusal to take such action appears to the court inconsistent with substantial justice. The court at every stage of the proceeding must disregard any error or defect in the proceeding which does not affect the substantial rights of the parties

Rule 62. Stay of proceedings to enforce a judgment

(A) Execution. Execution may issue upon notation of a judgment in the Chronological Case Summary except as otherwise provided in this rule hereinafter. During the pendency of an appeal the provisions of subdivision (C) of this rule govern the suspending, modifying, restoring, or granting of an injunction, the appointment of a receiver or, to the extent that a stay is not otherwise permitted by law upon appeal, any judgment or order for specific relief other than the payment of money.

(B) Stay of execution. In its discretion and on such conditions for the security of the adverse party as are proper, the court may stay the execution of or any proceedings to enforce a judgment pending the filing and disposition of

(1) a motion to correct error or to alter or amend a judgment made pursuant to Rule 59,

(2) a motion for judgment in accordance with a motion for a judgment on the evidence made pursuant to Rule 50,

(3) a motion for amendment to the findings or for additional findings or for a new trial or judgment made pursuant to Rule 52,

(4) a motion for relief from a judgment or order made pursuant to Rule 60, or

(5) an appeal.

(C) Stay of orders relating to injunctions, appointment of receivers and orders for specific relief. When an appeal is taken from an interlocutory or final judgment granting, dissolving or denying an injunction, the appointment of a receiver or, to the extent that a stay is not otherwise permitted by law upon appeal, from any judgment or order for specific relief other than the payment of money, the court to which the application is made in its sound discretion may suspend, modify, restore, or grant the injunction, the appointment of the receiver or the specific relief during the pendency of the appeal upon such terms as to bond or otherwise as it considers proper for the security of the rights of the adverse party. Nothing in this rule is intended to affect the original jurisdiction of the Supreme Court or the Indiana Court of Appeals.

(D) Stay upon appeal.

(1) Procedure for obtaining. No appeal bond or other security shall be necessary to perfect an appeal from any judgment or appealable interlocutory order. Enforcement of a judgment or appealable interlocutory order will be suspended during an appeal upon the giving of an adequate appeal bond with approved sureties, an irrevocable letter of credit from a financial institution approved in all respects by the court, or other form of security approved by the court. The bond, letter of credit, or other security may be given at or after the time of filing the notice of appeal. The stay is effective when the appeal bond, letter of credit, or other form of security is approved by the appropriate court. The trial court or judge shall have jurisdiction to fix and approve the bond or letter of credit and order a stay pending an appeal as well as prior to the appeal. If the stay is denied by the trial court the appellate tribunal may reconsider the application at any time after denial; and this provision also shall apply to stays or relief allowed under subdivision (C) of this rule. When the stay or relief is granted by the court on appeal, the clerk of the Supreme Court shall issue a certificate thereof to the clerk of the court below who shall file it with the judgment or order below and deliver it to the sheriff or any officer to whom execution or an enforcement order has been issued.

(2) Form of appeal bond or letter of credit. Whenever a party entitled thereto desires a stay on appeal, such party may present to the appropriate court for its approval an appeal bond or an irrevocable letter of credit from a financial institution. The bond or letter of credit shall be conditioned for the satisfaction of the judgment in full together with costs, interest, and damages for delay, if for any reason the appeal is dismissed or if the judgment is affirmed, and to satisfy in full such modification of the judgment and such

costs, interest, and damages as the appellate court may adjudge and award. When the judgment is for the recovery of money not otherwise secured, the amount of the bond or letter of credit shall be fixed at such sum as will cover the whole amount of the judgment remaining unsatisfied, costs on the appeal, interest, and damages for delay, unless the court after notice and hearing and for good cause shown fixes a different amount or orders security other than a bond or letter of credit. When the judgment determines the disposition of the property in controversy as in real action, replevin, and actions to foreclose liens or when such property is in the custody of the sheriff or when the proceeds of such property or a bond or letter of credit for its value is in the custody or control of the court, the amount of the appeal bond or letter of credit shall be fixed at such sum only as will secure the amount recovered for the use and detention of the property, the costs of the action, costs on appeal, interest, and damages for delay.

(3) Effect of appeal bond or letter of credit. Nothing in this subdivision shall be construed as giving the right to stay, by giving such bond or letter of credit, any judgment or order which cannot now be stayed or suspended by the giving of an appeal bond, except as provided in subdivisions (A), (B) and (C) of this rule. The provisions in this rule do not limit any power of an appellate court or of a judge or justice thereof to stay proceedings during the pendency of an appeal or to suspend, modify, restore, or grant an injunction during the pendency of an appeal or to make any order appropriate to preserve the status quo or the effectiveness of the judgment subsequently to be entered.

(E) Stay in favor of governmental organization--Personal representative. When an appeal or review is taken by a governmental organization, or by a court-appointed representative of a decedent's estate, guardian, receiver, assignee for the benefit of creditors, trustee or other court-appointed representative, the operation or enforcement of the judgment shall be stayed as it would as against other persons upon application to the appropriate court, but no bond, obligation or other security shall be required.

(F) Stay of execution under existing laws--Other bonds required before or as a condition to judgment: Money in lieu of bonds--Amount fixed by court. Execution upon a judgment for recovery of money or sale of property may be stayed, and personal property taken in execution may be delivered up as now provided by law. Indiana Acts, ch. 38, §§ 493-506 and §§ 531-536 (Spec.Sess.1881). [FN1] Nothing in this rule is intended to alter the right of a party to the protection of a surety bond or security or to obtain relief by furnishing a surety bond or security before or as a condition of final judgment, including without limitation such protection or relief in replevin, ejectment, attachment and injunction actions, upon judicial review of administrative action, in suits upon a lost instrument, for costs and the like. In any case where a surety bond, letter of credit, or security is furnished under this rule, the right to furnish money or a check in lieu of a bond shall remain unimpaired. Any requirement that the amount of the bond or letter of credit be fixed and reconsidered by the court in civil actions and proceedings shall remain unaffected by this rule.

(G) Effect of stay or temporary relief when new trial granted. When an appealable judgment or order is entered against a party who has obtained a prior stay or temporary relief by furnishing a surety bond, letter of credit, or other security, including without limitation relief in replevin, ejectment, attachment and injunctive actions, such stay or temporary relief shall lapse except to the extent:

(1) provided in subdivision (A) of this rule; or

(2) a stay is granted as provided or recognized in this rule.

If thereafter the order or judgment is reversed and a new trial or new hearing in fact is ordered or authorized in favor of such party, the original stay or relief shall not be reinstated unless the reversing court orders otherwise or, in the absence of such order, the court on the new trial or new hearing orders otherwise. When a stay or temporary relief is granted to a party seeking reversal of an appealable order or judgment under subdivision (B), (C) or (D) of this rule and a new trial or new hearing in fact is ordered or authorized in favor of such party, the stay or temporary relief shall continue until a final, appealable judgment or order is entered unless the court on review or appeal orders otherwise or, in the absence of such order, the court on the new trial or new hearing orders otherwise. Nothing in this subdivision is intended to limit the liability of the bondsman, the financial institution issuing the letter of credit, or other security or determine the order of liability assumed among different bondsmen or different security furnished in the course of proceedings before judgment, after judgment and after appeal or review.

(H) Stay of judgment as to multiple claims or multiple parties. When a court has ordered a final judgment under the conditions stated in Rule 54(B), the court may stay enforcement of that judgment until the entering of a subsequent judgment or judgments and may prescribe such conditions as are necessary to secure the benefit thereof to the party in whose favor the judgment is entered.

Rule 63. Disability and unavailability of a judge

(A) Disability and unavailability after the trial or hearing. The judge who presides at the trial of a cause or a hearing at which evidence is received shall, if available, hear motions and make all decisions and rulings required to be made by the court relating to the evidence and the conduct of the trial or hearing after the trial or hearing is concluded. If the judge before whom the trial or hearing was held is not available by reason of death, sickness, absence or unwillingness to act, then any other judge regularly sitting in the judicial circuit or assigned to the cause may perform any of the duties to be performed by the court after the verdict is returned or the findings or decision of the court is filed; but if he is satisfied that he cannot perform those duties because he did not preside at the trial or for any other reason, he may in his discretion grant a new trial or new hearing, in whole or in part. The unavailability of any such trial or hearing judge shall be determined and shown by a court order made by the successor judge at any time.

(B) Judge pro tempore in case of disability, unavailability, or neglect.

(1) When a judge of a court submits a verified petition and supporting proof to the Supreme Court stating that the judge is or will be unable to perform the duties of the office because of disability or other basis (e.g., order to military active duty), the Supreme Court shall promptly consider the petition.

(2) When a person submits a verified petition to the Supreme Court stating that a judge of a court (a) is unable to perform the duties of the office because of disability or (b) has failed, refused, or neglected to perform these duties, the Supreme Court shall issue an order to the judge, accompanied by the petition, requiring the judge to show cause as to why a judge pro tempore should not be appointed to perform the duties of the office. The order shall set a date for response and indicate that the judge may request a hearing. The order may include a date for such a hearing on or after the date set for response. The order shall be served at least ten (10) days before the date set for response.

(3) If the Supreme Court is satisfied that a petition submitted under subsection (1) or (2) should be granted, it shall appoint a full-time judge pro tempore to perform the duties of the office until (a) the term of the office is ended, (b) the office becomes vacant, or (c) the judge's ability to resume those duties is established.

(4) A judge who seeks to resume the duties of the office shall submit a verified petition and supporting proof to the Supreme Court. The judge may request a hearing on the petition.

(5) The Supreme Court may order a judge who has submitted a petition under subsection (1) to demonstrate that the judge is or remains unable to perform the duties of the office.

(C) Qualifications and authority of a judge pro tempore. Any judge appointed under this or any other rule or law shall be an attorney in good standing at the bar of the Supreme Court of this state. In the event the Supreme Court of the state shall appoint a judge pro tempore under these provisions, a duly certified copy of the order and judgment of appointment of such judge pro tempore, attested by the chief justice, shall be issued to the person so appointed. If the person so appointed consents to serve, he shall be qualified as other judges are qualified. A certified copy of the order and judgment of appointment shall be filed with the clerk of the named court and entered in the appropriate records of said court. The person so appointed and qualified as a judge pro tempore shall perform the duties of the regular judge of the court, but always shall be subject to the continuing jurisdiction of the Supreme Court. In the event any judge pro tempore, appointed under the provisions of this rule shall fail to qualify and assume the duties of the regular judge of such court, or in the event such judge pro tempore fails to conduct the business of the court as provided by law, the clerk of the court shall notify the Supreme Court in writing of this fact. Upon the receipt of such notification, the Supreme Court may take such action in the premises, in order to further the administration of justice, as such court may deem to be necessary and just.

(D) Compensation of judge pro tempore. A judge pro tempore appointed by the Supreme Court under this rule shall receive a salary computed at the same rate as the regular judge commencing from the date he qualifies. A judge pro tempore appointed locally shall be paid twenty-five dollars $25.00 for each day or part thereof actually served. The judge pro tempore shall be paid out of the respective county, city or town general fund, without an appropriation therefor, upon allowance by the board of county commissioners of the county or council of the city or town in which the court is located. If he is appointed locally, the judge pro tempore shall present a claim to the board of county commissioners specifying the number of days or parts of days actually served, which claim shall be verified by the clerk of the court and the board shall allow the claim. If he is appointed by the Supreme Court, the judge shall present a claim to the board with a copy of his appointment from the Supreme Court, a statement showing the date of his qualification verified by the clerk and a request that he be paid in the same manner thereafter as a regular judge, and thereafter he shall be paid in the same manner as a regular judge. Nothing herein shall be construed to diminish in any manner the compensation of any regular judge so long as such regular judge continues in office.

(E) Judge pro tempore when judge is unable to attend. A judge who is unable to attend and preside at his court for any cause may appoint in writing a judge pro tempore to conduct the business of this court during his absence. The written appointment shall be entered in the records of the court. When duly sworn, or without being sworn if he is a judge of a court of this state, the judge pro tempore shall have the same authority during the period of his appointment as the judge he replaces. A judge appointed under this provision must meet the qualifications prescribed in subdivision (C) of this rule. Such judge shall be allowed the sum of $25.00 for each day or part thereof actually served, per diem as provided in Rule 79(P) and in the manner provided by subdivision (D) of this rule. In his absence or when he shall be unable to make such appointment, the appointment may be made by the clerk of his court, or the deputy clerk assigned to his court or in his absence by any available county officer.

ule 63.1. Lis pendens notice of proceedings avoiding judgments and circumstances tolling and xtending statutes of limitations; assignments and discharges in lis pendens and judgment dockets; lis endens notices in cases involving interest in personal property

(A) Lis pendens notice of avoidance of judgment and tolling of statute of limitations--Effect of failure to file notice thereof. Avoidance of, or proceedings to avoid a final judgment by a subsequent motion for judgment on the evidence (Rule 50), for amendment of the finding or judgment (Rule 52), and to correct errors (Rule 59), by proceedings for relief from a judgment under Rule 60(B) or under the appellate rules and the tolling or extension of the statute of limitations or other bar of a claim to the property shall be ineffective against a purchaser of an interest in land or a purchaser or lien creditor who acquires an interest in personal property and who claims such interest under or because of such judgment, such tolling or such extension if:

(1) the purchaser of land gives value and perfects of record or takes possession of the land in good faith and without notice of the avoidance, tolling or extension while the person against whom he claims is not in possession of the land and before he has filed notice in the lis pendens record of the county where the land is located; or

(2) the purchaser or lien creditor acquiring an interest in personal property, as a buyer, would take priority over an unperfected security interest while the person against whom he claims has not perfected by possession and before he has filed a financing statement containing lis pendens notice as provided in subdivision (C) of this rule.

The lis pendens notice shall be signed by the party or his attorney seeking avoidance of the judgment or the party with the claim asserted to be tolled; identify the judgment by court and docket number; describe the claim in terms which will lead to the records where any evidence thereof is filed or recorded if such is the case; name the parties; in the case of land designate a present record owner thereof if the parties named are not such owner or owners; and describe the land or personal property if the judgment or claim relates to described land or personal property.

(B) Satisfactions and assignments of docketed judgments and matters entered in lis pendens record. A satisfaction, dismissal, release or assignment of claims or matters recorded or filed in the lis pendens record relating to land or of a judgment entered in the judgment docket may be filed or recorded and indexed in the same manner as originally filed, recorded or docketed, and for the same fees provided that such satisfaction, dismissal, release or assignment is:

(1) in writing, describing the judgment by cause number, signed by the person executing it and acknowledged as in the case of a deed; or

(2) in writing certified as entered in his records by the clerk of court where the judgment is entered or the action is pending;

(3) entered in writing upon the margin of the record signed by the person executing it and attested by the clerk's signature.

A satisfaction, continuation, dismissal, release or assignment of a lis pendens notice filed in the case of personal property is sufficient if it meets the requirements of a termination statement, continuation statement, assignment or release of a financing statement.

(C) Constructive notice of lis pendens against personal property and rights of lien creditors. Judicial proceedings brought by a creditor to enforce an unperfected interest in personal property and a lien obtained by judicial proceedings (including tax and other liens through judicial records) in personal property shall not serve as constructive or lis pendens notice thereof until possession is acquired by the creditor or by a court officer, or until notice thereof by the creditor is perfected by filing a financing statement:

(1) naming the defendant as debtor, and the creditor as secured party;

(2) briefly describing the collateral in such words as a "lien upon debtor's personal property by judicial proceedings" and indicating the kind or type of property, along with the court and cause number of the action;

(3) signed by the creditor or judgment creditor; and

(4) in the filing office or offices where a financing statement under a security agreement with respect to the collateral, if filed, would be required to be filed.

Lis pendens notice under this provision is subject to principles of estoppel or commercial law governing negotiable instruments and documents, securities or quasi-negotiable instruments or documents; and to the provisions of Article 9 the Uniform Commercial Code [FN1] relating to the duration of filing. In an appropriate case the debtor or judgment debtor shall be entitled to a termination statement when judgment in his favor becomes final or when the lien obtained by judicial proceedings is terminated or is satisfied, as in the case of a debtor under a security agreement.

(D) Effect of judgment on lis pendens notice. A properly filed lis pendens notice of a claim against property continues to be perfected with respect to a judgment establishing such claim for the duration of the judgment, subject to the duration of filing under subdivision (C) of this rule.

[FN1] IC 26-1-9-101 et seq.

Rule 64. Seizure of person or property

(A) Ancillary remedies to assist in enforcement of judgment.

(1) At the commencement of and during the course of an action, all remedies providing for seizure of person or property for the purpose of securing satisfaction of the judgment ultimately to be entered in the action are available under the circumstances and in the manner provided by law and existing at the time the remedy is sought. The remedies thus available include, without limitation, arrest, attachment, attachment and garnishment, lis pendens notice, ejectment, replevin, sequestration, and other corresponding or equivalent legal or equitable remedies, however designated and regardless of whether by existing procedure the remedy is ancillary to an action or must be obtained by an independent action. Such remedies are subject to the provisions of this rule, and, except as herein otherwise provided, the action in which any of the foregoing remedies is used shall be commenced and prosecuted pursuant to these rules.

(2) The court may issue a writ of attachment, bench warrant, or body attachment if:

(a) a rule to show cause has been issued by the court and served upon the judgment debtor by delivering a copy of the same to the judgment debtor personally. Personal service under this rule includes certified mail signed by the judgment debtor;

(b) if service is not made in open court, the person making service has filed a return or affidavit stating that personal service was made upon the judgement debtor and setting forth the time, place, and manner thereof; and

(c) the judgment debtor has failed to appear at the rule to show cause hearing as ordered.

In addition to statutory requirements, the writ of attachment, bench warrant, or body attachment shall contain sufficient information to identify the judgment debtor.

(3) A person taken into custody in a civil action must be brought before the court that issued the writ, bench warrant or body attachment, or before a judicial officer having jurisdiction over the person within forty-eight (48) hours, excluding weekends and holidays, following the person being taken into custody. The person shall be advised of the procedures for release, including any bond, escrow amount set by the issuing court in the writ, bench warrant or body attachment.

(B) Attachment or attachment and garnishment. Attachment or attachment and garnishment shall be allowed in the following cases in addition to those where such remedies prior to judgment are now permitted by law:

(1) It shall be a cause for attachment that the defendant or one of several defendants is a foreign corporation, a nonresident of this state, or a person whose residence and whereabouts are unknown and cannot be determined after reasonable investigation before the commencement of the action.

(2) Any interest in tangible or intangible property owned by the defendant shall be subject to attachment or attachment and garnishment, as the case may be, if it is subject to execution, proceedings supplemental to execution or any creditor process allowed by law. Wages or salaries shall not be subject to pre-judgment attachment and garnishment, except as otherwise provided by law.

(3) Attachment or attachment and garnishment shall be allowed in favor of the plaintiff suing upon a claim for money, whether founded on contract, tort, equity or any other theory and whether it is liquidated, contingent or unliquidated; or upon a claim to determine the rights in the property or obligation attached or garnisheed.

(4) It shall not be objectionable that the property or obligation being attached or garnisheed is in the possession of the plaintiff or is owing by the plaintiff to the defendant or by the defendant to the plaintiff.

(5) A governmental organization, or a representative, including a guardian, receiver, assignee for the benefit of creditors, trustee or representative of a decedent's estate may be named as a garnishee and bound by the duties of a garnishee.

(6) A writ of attachment against the defendant's real estate or his interest therein is effectively served by recordation of notice of the action in the appropriate lis pendens record, and, unless vacant, by serving the writ of attachment or notice thereof upon a person in possession of the land.

(C) Defendant's title raised by denial--Effect of dismissal. In action where the plaintiff is required to establish title to any fund or property, including without limitation any ejectment, replevin, quiet title, partition, equitable, legal or other action, the defendant in his answer may deny the plaintiff's claim of title and thereby place in issue the defendant's title or interest therein. If the defendant prevails under such an answer he shall be entitled to a judgment or decree enunciating his title or interest and any proper negative or affirmative relief against the plaintiff consistent with his proof.

Unless the defendant joins in the notice of dismissal, no voluntary dismissal by the plaintiff in such cases shall be allowed without prejudice after the plaintiff has obtained possession of the property or fund or other relief with respect thereto by posting bond, or after the defendant by answer (whether by denial, affirmative defense, counter-claim or cross-claim) has placed title in issue.

Rule 65. Injunctions

(A) Preliminary injunction.

(1) Notice. No preliminary injunction shall be issued without an opportunity for a hearing upon notice to the adverse party.

(2) Consolidation of hearing with trial on merits. Before or after the commencement of the hearing of an application for a preliminary injunction, the court may order the trial of the action on the merits to be advanced and consolidated with the hearing of the application. Even when this consolidation is not ordered, any evidence received upon an application for a preliminary injunction which would be admissible upon the trial on the merits becomes part of the record on the trial and need not be repeated upon the trial.

(3) Assignment of cases--Judge to act promptly. Assignment of cases shall not be affected by the fact that a temporary restraining order or preliminary injunction is sought, but such case shall be assigned promptly and the judge regularly assigned to the case shall act upon and hear all matters relating to temporary restraining orders and preliminary injunctions. The judge shall make himself readily available to consider temporary restraining orders, conduct hearings, fix the manner of giving notice and the time and place for hearings under this rule, and shall act and require the parties to act promptly.

If the party seeking relief or his attorney by affidavit establishes that the judge assigned to the case is not available or cannot be found to consider an application for a restraining order, to conduct a hearing, or to fix the manner of giving notice and the time and place for a hearing under this rule, he may apply to any other judge in the circuit who shall take all further action with respect to any temporary restraining order or preliminary injunction. If the affidavit establishes that no other judge in the circuit is available or to be found, he may apply to the judge of any adjoining circuit. Unless an order is entered within ten [10] days after the hearing upon the granting, modifying or dissolving of a temporary or preliminary injunction, the relief sought shall be subject to the provisions of Rule 53.1.

(4) Modification of orders--Responsive pleadings. Upon the court's own motion or the motion of any party, orders granting or denying temporary restraining orders or preliminary injunctions may be dissolved, modified, granted or reinstated. Responsive pleadings shall not be required in response to any pleadings or motions relating to temporary restraining orders or preliminary injunctions.

(B) Temporary restraining order--Notice--Hearing--Duration. A temporary restraining order may be granted without written or oral notice to the adverse party or his attorney only if:

(1) it clearly appears from specific facts shown by affidavit or by the verified complaint that immediate and irreparable injury, loss, or damage will result to the applicant before the adverse party or his attorney can be heard in opposition; and

(2) the applicant's attorney certifies to the court in writing the efforts, if any, which have been made to give notice and the reasons supporting his claim that notice should not be required.

Every temporary restraining order granted without notice shall be indorsed with the date and hour of issuance; shall be filed forthwith in the clerk's office and entered of record; shall define the injury and state why it is irreparable and why the order was granted without notice; and shall expire by its terms within such time after entry, not to exceed ten [10] days, as the court fixes, unless within the time so fixed the order, for good cause shown, is extended for a like period or unless the whereabouts of the party against whom the order is granted is unknown and cannot be determined by reasonable diligence or unless the party against whom the order is directed consents that it may be extended for a longer period. The reasons for the extension shall be entered of record. In case a temporary restraining order is granted without notice, the motion for a preliminary injunction shall be set down for hearing at the earliest possible time and takes precedence of all matters except older matters of the same character; and when the motion comes on for hearing the party who obtained the temporary restraining order shall proceed with the application for a preliminary injunction and, if he does not do so, the court shall dissolve the temporary restraining order. On two (2) days' notice to the party who obtained the temporary restraining order without notice or on such shorter notice to that party as the court may prescribe, the adverse party may appear and move its dissolution or modification and in that event the court shall proceed to hear and determine such motion as expeditiously as the ends of justice require.

(C) Security. No restraining order or preliminary injunction shall issue except upon the giving of security by the applicant, in such sum as the court deems proper, for the payment of such costs and damages as may be incurred or suffered by any party who is found to have been wrongfully enjoined or restrained. No such security shall be required of a governmental organization, but such governmental organization shall be responsible for costs and damages as may be incurred or suffered by any party who is found to have been wrongfully enjoined or restrained.

The provisions of Rule 65.1 apply to a surety upon a bond or undertaking under this rule.

(D) Form and scope of injunction or restraining order. Every order granting temporary injunction and every restraining order shall include or be accompanied by findings as required by Rule 52; shall be specific in terms; shall describe in reasonable detail, and not by reference to the complaint or other document, the act or acts sought to be restrained; and is binding only upon the parties to the action, their officers, agents, servants, employees, and attorneys, and upon those persons in active concert or participation with them who receive actual notice of the order by personal service or otherwise.

(E) Temporary Restraining Orders--Domestic Relations Cases. Parties wishing protection from domestic or family violence in Domestic Relations cases shall petition the court pursuant to IC 34-26-5. Subject to the provisions set forth in this paragraph, in an action for dissolution of marriage, separation, or child support, the court may issue a Temporary Restraining Order, without hearing or security, if either party files a verified petition alleging an injury would result to the moving party if no immediate order were issued.

(1) Joint Order. If the court finds that an order shall be entered under this paragraph, the court may enjoin both parties from:

(a) transferring, encumbering, concealing, selling or otherwise disposing of any joint property of the parties or asset of the marriage except in the usual course of business or for the necessities of life, without the written consent of the parties of the permission of the court; and/or

(b) removing any child of the parties then residing in the State of Indiana from the State with the intent to deprive the court of jurisdiction over such child without the prior written consent of all parties or the permission of the court.

(2) Separate Order Required. In the event a party seeks to enjoin by a temporary restraining order the non-moving party from abusing, harassing, or disturbing the peace of the petitioning party or any child or step-child of the parties, or exclude the non-moving party from the family dwelling, the dwelling of the non-moving party, or any other place, and the court determines that an order shall be issued, such order shall be addressed to one person. A joint or mutual restraining order shall not be issued. If both parties allege injury, they shall do so by separate petitions. The trial court shall review each petition separately and grant or deny each petition on its individual merits. In the event the trial court finds cause to grant both petitions, it shall do so by separate orders.

(3) Effect of Order. An order entered under this paragraph is automatically effective upon service. Such orders are enforceable by all remedies provided by law including contempt. Once issued, such orders remain in effect until the entry of a decree or final order or until modified or dissolved by the court.

(F) Statutory Provision Unaffected by this Rule. Nothing in this rule shall affect provisions of statutes extending or limiting the power of a court to grant injunctions. By way of example and not by way of limitation, this rule shall not affect the provisions of 1967 Indiana Acts, ch. 357, §§ 1-8 [FN1] relating to public lawsuits, and Indiana Acts, ch. 7, §§ 1-15 [FN2] providing for removal of injunctive and mandamus actions to the Court of Appeals of Indiana, and Indiana Acts, ch. 12 (1933).

ule 65.1. Security: Proceedings against sureties

/henever these rules or other laws require or permit the giving of security by a party to a court action or proceeding, and ecurity is given in the form of a bond or stipulation or other undertaking with one or more sureties, each surety submits imself to the jurisdiction of the court and irrevocably appoints the clerk of the court as his agent upon whom any papers ffecting his liability on the bond or undertaking may be served. His liability may be enforced on motion without the ecessity of an independent action. The motion and such notice of the motion as the court prescribes may be served on the lerk of the court, who shall forthwith mail copies to the sureties if their addresses are known. This rule applies to bonds r security furnished on appeal, and enforcement shall be in the court to which the case is returned after appeal.

ule 66. Receivers, assignees for the benefit of creditors and statutory and other liquidators; claims gainst such officers

(A) Actions; appointment; procedure. An action wherein a receiver, assignee for the benefit of creditors or statutory, or other liquidator has been appointed shall not be dismissed except by order of the court. Administration of such estates shall be in accordance with the practice heretofore followed. In all other respects the action in which the appointment of such officer is sought or which is brought by or against him is governed by these rules.

(B) Statement of assets and liabilities. Whenever a receiver, assignee for the benefit of creditors, statutory or other liquidator shall have been appointed to take over the business or assets of any person, organization, or partnership, the court appointing such officer may, or upon petition of any interested person shall, fix a time within which the person, or members, owners, agents or officers of the business or assets so placed in the hands of the officer, shall file with the clerk of the court in which such proceedings are had, a full, complete, itemized statement in affidavit form, setting forth in detail all the assets and all the liabilities of such person, organization or partnership including a list of the names and addresses of all known creditors. In case of noncompliance, the statement shall be prepared by the liquidator.

(C) Notice of appointment--Time within which to file claims. After such statement is filed, such officer shall give reasonable notice of his appointment by publication as ordered by the court, and the receiver shall mail a copy of said notice to all creditors listed on the statement so filed or prepared. Said notice shall state the date of appointment of the receiver and the period of time, as shall have been fixed by the court, within which creditors may file claims. Said period of time shall not be less than six [6] months from said date of appointment.

(D) Claims. The procedure for the filing, consideration, allowance or trial of claims in receiverships and assignments for the benefit of creditors, or statutory or other liquidations, shall, insofar as is practicable, conform with the procedure relating to claims in decedents' estates.

(E) Claims which must be paid without filing. A receiver, assignee for the benefit of creditors, statutory or other liquidator shall pay or make distributions according to priorities as required by law upon all claims, whether properly filed or filed within the allowed time after the appointment of the officer, if:

(1) liquidated in amount or capable of liquidation by a mathematical computation;

(2) the claim was owing and could have been filed and proved after the officer's appointment; and

(3) it is shown to be unpaid or owing upon the books or records of the debtor regularly and currently maintained for the purpose of showing the status of claims of such class.

Payment or distribution hereunder may be recovered by the officer or his successor to the extent it was excessive, not owing, or not payable. Upon petition of any interested person or the officer prior to final distribution or along with a petition for final distribution, the court may determine the existence or nonexistence of claims subject to this subdivision and may issue appropriate orders for payment or nonpayment as the case may be.

Rule 67. Deposit in court; payment of judgment

(A) Deposit in court before judgment. Before judgment in an action in which any part of the relief sought is a judgment for a sum of money or the disposition of a sum of money or the disposition of any other thing capable of delivery, a party, upon notice to every other party, and by leave of court, may deposit with the court all or any part of such sum or thing. Payment of all or part thereof may be directed by the court under any judgment or order, or upon motion and hearing to the rightful owners or upon security or agreement of the parties under the direction of the court.

(B) Payment of judgment--Satisfaction entered of record. Unless otherwise directed by the court, payment of money owing under and following a judgment may be made to the judgment creditor or his attorney, to the sheriff holding a writ of execution, or to the clerk of the court where the judgment is rendered. If paid to the clerk, the clerk shall notify the person entitled thereto or his attorney and shall pay such sum to him upon receiving a statement of satisfaction required herein. Money received by the sheriff towards satisfaction of the judgment shall be delivered to the clerk of the court where the judgment is rendered who shall then proceed as the money were paid to him. A party or person receiving payment or satisfaction of a judgment shall furnish to the sheriff, clerk, party or person making payment a signed statement of total or partial satisfaction and any necessary assignment identifying the judgment by cause number and acknowledged as in the case of a deed which, when acquired or delivered to the clerk shall be entered in the records with the judgment. Such statement or any other entry by the clerk showing an assignment, payment or satisfaction of the judgment when certified by the clerk shall be received as evidence thereof, may be filed in the lis pendens record or judgment docket as provided in Rule 63.1(B) and when so filed shall serve as constructive notice thereof.

Rule 68. Offer of judgment

At any time more than ten [10] days before the trial begins, a party defending against a claim may serve upon the adverse party an offer to allow judgment to be taken against him for the money or property or to the effect specified in his offer, with costs then accrued. If within ten [10] days after the service of the offer the adverse party serves written notice that the offer is accepted, either party may then file the offer and notice of acceptance together with proof of service thereof and thereupon the clerk shall enter judgment. An offer not accepted shall be deemed withdrawn and evidence thereof is not admissible except in a proceeding to determine costs. If the judgment finally obtained by the offeree is not more favorable than the offer, the offeree must pay the costs incurred after the making of the offer. The fact that an offer is made but not accepted does not preclude a subsequent offer. When liability of one party to another has been partially determined by verdict or order of judgment, but the amount or extent of liability remains to be determined by further proceedings, the party adjudged liable may make an offer of judgment, which shall have the same effect as an offer made before trial if it is served within a reasonable time not less than ten [10] days prior to the commencement of hearings to determine the amount or extent of liability.

Rule 69. Execution, proceedings supplemental to execution, foreclosure sales

(A) Execution sales. Process to enforce a judgment or a decree for the payment of money shall be by writ of execution, unless the court directs otherwise and except as provided herein. Notwithstanding any statute to the contrary, real estate shall not be sold until the elapse of six [6] months from the time the judgment or execution thereon becomes a lien upon the property.

The sale of real estate shall be conducted under the same rules and the same procedures applicable to foreclosure of mortgages, including subdivision (C) of this rule, without right of redemption after the sale but subject to the judgment debtor's right to care for and remove crops growing at the time the lien attached as in the case of mortgage foreclosure. Unless otherwise ordered by the court, the sheriff or person conducting the sale of any property upon execution shall not be required to offer it for sale in any particular order, in parcels, or first offer rents and profits and shall be required to sell real and personal property separately pursuant to the law applicable. Execution upon any property shall not suspend the right and duty to levy upon other property.

(B) Judgment and execution liens on after-acquired property. In the case of property acquired by the debtor after prior judgment or execution liens have been perfected, such liens shall share pro rata with each other without further levy.

(C) Foreclosure of liens upon real estate. Unless otherwise ordered by the court, judicial foreclosure of all liens upon real estate shall be conducted under the same rules and the same procedures applicable to foreclosure of mortgages upon real estate, including without limitation redemption rights, manner and notice of sale, appointment of a receiver, execution of deed to purchaser and without valuation and appraisement. Judicial lien foreclosures including mortgage foreclosures may be held at any reasonable place stated in the notice of sale. In all cases where a foreclosure or execution sale of realty is not confirmed by the court, the sheriff or other officer conducting the sale shall make a record of his actions therein in his return to be filed promptly with the record of the case and also in the execution docket maintained in the office of the clerk.

(D) Other judicial sales. Unless otherwise ordered by the court all public judicial sales of real estate, other than lien and mortgage foreclosures and execution sales, shall, to the extent possible, be sold in the same manner that real estate is sold in the administration of decedents' estates, and subject to the same rules applicable to the manner and effect thereof. This provision shall apply, without limitation, to judicial sales by trustees, guardians, receivers, assignees for the benefit of creditors and sales in partition proceedings.

(E) Proceedings supplemental to execution. Notwithstanding any other statute to the contrary, proceedings supplemental to execution may be enforced by verified motion or with affidavits in the court where the judgment is rendered alleging generally:

(1) that the plaintiff owns the described judgment against the defendant;

(2) that the plaintiff has no cause to believe that levy of execution against the defendant will satisfy the judgment;

(3) that the defendant be ordered to appear before the court to answer as to his non-exempt property subject to execution or proceedings supplemental to execution or to apply any such specified or unspecified property towards satisfaction of the judgment; and,

(4) if any person is named as garnishee, that garnishee has or will have specified or unspecified nonexempt property of, or an obligation owing to the judgment debtor subject to execution or proceedings supplemental to execution, and that the garnishee be ordered to appear and answer concerning the same or answer interrogatories submitted with the motion.

If the court determines that the motion meets the foregoing requirements it shall, ex parte and without notice, order the judgment debtor, other named parties defendant and the garnishee to appear for a hearing thereon or to answer the interrogatories attached to the motion, or both.

The motion, along with the court's order stating the time for the appearance and hearing or the time for the answer to interrogatories submitted with the motion, shall be served upon the judgment debtor as provided in Rule 5, and other parties and the garnishee shall be entitled to service of process as provided in Rule 4. The date fixed for appearance and hearing or answer to interrogatories shall be not less than twenty [20] days after service. No further pleadings shall be required, and the case shall be heard and determined and property ordered applied towards the judgment in accordance with statutes allowing proceedings supplementary to execution. In aid of the judgment or execution, the judgment creditor or his successor in interest of record and the judgment debtor may utilize the discovery provisions of these rules in the manner provided in these rules for discovery or as provided under the laws allowing proceedings supplemental.

Writs of attachment, bench warrants, and body attachments are governed by Trial Rule 64(A).

(F) Title opinion or insurance required in all judicial sales of land. In the case of any judicial sale of land, including without limitation mortgage and lien foreclosures, execution sales, sales by receivers, assignees for the benefit of creditors, guardians or trustees, or partition sales, upon motion the court in its discretion may order the judgment creditor, person seeking the sale, or officer conducting the sale to procure a qualified title opinion or a title insurance policy from a title insurance company authorized to do business in Indiana with respect to the interest of the person whose land is being sold. The policy must be conditioned to cover the purchase price at the sale and may be given with any necessary exclusions. The opinion or policy shall run to all parties interested in the litigation and to any purchaser or purchasers at the sale. The opinion or policy or copy thereof shall be available for inspection in the court from which the sale is being conducted or in the office of the court officer conducting the sale at the first notice of sale and shall be made available for inspection at the sale. Expenses of the opinion or policy shall be taxed as costs like other expenses of the sale and paid from the first proceeds of the sale. The opinion or policy shall not cover defects arising in the conduct of the sale.

Rule 70. Judgment for specific acts; vesting title; recordation

(A) Effect of judgment. If a judgment directs a party to execute a conveyance of land, or other property or to deliver deeds or other documents or to perform any other specific act and the party fails to comply within the time specified, the court may direct the act to be done at the cost of the disobedient party by some other person appointed by the court and the act when so done has like effect as if done by the party. On application of the party entitled to performance, the clerk shall issue a writ of attachment, writ of assistance, or sequestration against the property of the disobedient party to compel obedience to the judgment. The court may also in proper cases adjudge the party in contempt and may award damages for disobedience of the order. If real or personal property is involved, the court in lieu of directing a conveyance thereof may enter a judgment divesting the title of any party and vesting it in others and such judgment has the effect of both a judgment and of a conveyance executed in due form of law.

When any order or judgment is for the delivery of possession, the party in whose favor it is entered is entitled to a writ of execution, assistance or order directing the sheriff or other enforcement officer to deliver possession upon application to the clerk. Equitable decrees or orders to pay money shall be enforced as legal judgments to pay money unless otherwise ordered by the court.

(B) Recordation of judgment. A copy of the judgment directing acts or divesting or vesting title of a deed or copy thereof transferring title as provided in subdivision (A) of this rule or other law may be recorded or filed either in the lis pendens records or the deed records of the proper officer and county or place and shall be appropriately indexed. When recorded or filed such record shall constitute constructive notice thereof in transactions with respect to the property under the recording laws, and a copy of such filed or recorded judgment or deed certified by the county recorder or other officer shall constitute prima facie evidence of its validity.

(C) Deed form. A conveyance of land made by a court appointee as authorized by subdivision (A) of this rule may be made in the following form:

"A B by the order (for judgment) of (naming the court), in cause number (state the cause number) entered on (state date order or judgment was entered), in the case of (naming the party plaintiffs) against (naming the party defendants) conveys the (describe the premises, and the interest conveyed if the judgment or order is for less than a fee simple absolute) the title, interest and rights of (name the parties or persons whose title is being conveyed; and the record owner through whom such title was derived if known and if such persons are not record owners), (state with warranty or subject to conditions only if and as provided in the order or judgment). Signed (signature of court appointee, A B), Appointee of above named court to make this conveyance." (Acknowledgment as required in the case of deeds.)

(D) Judicial sales. Property may be sold under judgments and orders in the manner now provided by law subject to these rules, including the sale of the property when specific performance is allowed against the vendee.

Rule 71. Process in behalf of and against persons not parties

When an order is made in favor of a person who is not a party to the action, he may enforce obedience to the order by the same process as if he were a party; and, when obedience to an order may be lawfully enforced against a person who is not a party, he is liable to the same process for enforcing obedience to the order as if he were a party.

Rule 72. Trial Court and Clerks

(A) Trial courts always open. The trial courts shall be deemed always open for the purpose of filing any pleading or other proper paper, of issuing and returning process and of making and directing all interlocutory motions, orders, and rules. Terms of court shall not be recognized.

(B) Trials and hearings--Orders in chambers. All trials upon the merits shall be conducted in open court and so far as convenient in a regular courtroom in or outside the county seat. All other acts or proceedings may be done or conducted by a judge in chambers, without the attendance of the clerk or other court officials and at any place either within or without the circuit; but, no hearing other than one ex parte, shall be conducted outside the state without the consent of all parties affected thereby.

(C) Clerk's office and orders by clerk. The clerk's office with the clerk or a deputy in attendance shall be open during business hours on all days except Saturdays, Sundays, and legal holidays, but the circuit court judge may provide by local rule or order that its clerk's office shall be open for specified hours on Saturdays or particular legal holidays other than New Year's Day, Washington's Birthday, Memorial Day, Independence Day, Labor Day, Veterans Day, Thanksgiving Day, and Christmas Day. All motions and applications in the clerk's office for issuing process, including final process to enforce and execute judgments, and for other proceedings which do not require allowance or order of the court are grantable of course by the clerk; but the clerk's action may be suspended or altered or rescinded by the court upon cause shown.

(D) Notice of Orders or Judgments. Immediately upon the notation in the Chronological Case Summary of a ruling upon a motion, an order or judgment, the clerk shall serve a copy of the entry in the manner provided for in Rule 5(B) upon each party who is not in default for failure to appear and shall make a record of such service. Such service is sufficient notice for all purposes for which notice of the entry is required by these rules; but any party may, in addition, serve a notice of such entry in the manner provided in Rule 5 for the service of papers. In cases of consolidated proceedings involving ten (10) or more parties, the trial judge may provide by order for alternative method of notice to designated liaison parties who undertake responsibility for forwarding notice to all parties.

It shall be the duty of the attorneys, and parties not represented by an attorney, when entering their appearance in a case or when filing pleadings or papers therein, to have noted on the Chronological Case Summary and on the pleadings or papers so filed, their mailing address, and an electronic mail address. Service at either address shall be deemed sufficient.

(E) Effect of Lack of Notice. Lack of notice, or the lack of the actual receipt of a copy of the entry from the Clerk shall not affect the time within which to contest the ruling, order or judgment, or authorize the Court to relieve a party of the failure to initiate proceedings to contest such ruling, order or judgment, except as provided in this section. When the service of a copy of the entry by the Clerk is not evidenced by a note made by the Clerk upon the Chronological Case Summary, the Court, upon application for good cause shown, may grant an extension of any time limitation within which to contest such ruling, order or judgment to any party who was without actual knowledge, or who relied upon incorrect representations by Court personnel. Such extension shall commence when the party first obtained actual knowledge and not exceed the original time limitation.

Rule 73. Hearing of motions

(A) [FN1] **Hearings upon motions.** Unless local conditions make it impracticable, each judge shall establish regular times and places, at intervals sufficiently frequent for the prompt dispatch of business, at which motions requiring notice and hearing may be heard and disposed of; but the judge at any time or place and on such notice, if any, as he considers reasonable may make order for the advancement, conduct, and hearing of actions. To expedite its business, the court may direct the submission and determination of motions without oral hearing upon brief written statements of reasons in support and opposition, or direct or permit hearings by telephone conference call with all attorneys or other similar means of communication.

FN1] This rule contains no Subd. (B).

Rule 74. Recording machines; court reports; stenographic report or transcript as evidence

(A) Recording machines--Transcripts. For the purpose of facilitating and expediting the trial of causes and the appeals therefrom, the judge of each circuit, criminal, superior, probate and juvenile court of each and every county of this state may arrange and provide for the recording by electronic or mechanical device, or by stenographic reporting with computer-aided transcription capability of, any and all oral evidence and testimony given in all causes and hearings, including both questions and answers, and all rulings of the judge in respect to the admission and rejection of evidence and objections thereto and the recording of any other oral matters occurring during the hearing in any proceeding. The recording device or the computer aided transcription equipment shall be selected and approved by the court and may be placed under the supervision and operation of the official court reporter or such other person as may be designated by the court. The court may, in its discretion, eliminate shorthand or stenographic reporting of any recorded matter.

A transcript, typewritten or in longhand, made in part or entirely from such recording, shall serve the same purpose as if made from shorthand notes and if certified, as in the case of a transcript of shorthand notes, shall serve the same purpose and be as valid as if made from shorthand notes.

Provided further, that the judge may authorize or direct the court reporter or any other responsible, competent person, in his discretion, to make a transcription from such recordings, and the same shall be certified by the person making said transcriptions in the same manner and have the same effect as if made from shorthand notes.

(B) Reporter may serve as clerk and serve other judges. When the circuit court judge and the judge or judges affected find that such duties will not affect the efficiency of the court, one [1] person may serve both as a court reporter and clerk for a judge or judges whose regular courtroom is located outside the courthouse or its environs; and a court reporter may serve more than one [1] judge. Appointment shall be made by the judge or judges affected and, if they cannot agree, by the circuit court judge.

(C) Pay and duties of court reporters. It shall be the duty of each court reporter whenever required by the judge, to be promptly present in court, and take down in shorthand or by other means the oral evidence given in all causes, including both questions and answers, and to note all rulings of the judge in respect to the admission and rejection of evidence and the objections and exceptions thereto, and write out the instructions of the court in jury trials. The court reporter, when so directed, shall record the proceedings and make a transcript as provided in subdivision (A) of this rule. Reporters shall be paid as provided by 1965 Indiana Acts, ch. 289 [FN1], but the circuit court judge with the approval of the judge or judges affected may allow the reporter additional pay up to $125 per month for serving more than one [1] judge or function, or serving as both clerk and reporter.

(D) Statutes applicable to reporters and preparation of transcripts. Except as provided otherwise by these rules, the provisions of 1899 Indiana Acts, ch. 169, §§ 2-7, [FN2] 1939 Indiana Acts, ch. 11, § 1, [FN3] 1935 Indiana Acts, ch. 218, § 1, [FN4] 1893 Indiana Acts, ch. 33, § 1, [FN5] and 1947 Indiana Acts, ch. 89, § 1, [FN6] relating to court reporters and preparation of transcripts, shall apply to court reporters provided by these rules.

(E) Stenographic report or transcript as evidence. Whenever the testimony of a witness at a trial or hearing which was stenographically reported is admissible on appeal or in evidence at a later trial, proceeding, or administrative hearing, it may be proved by the transcript thereof duly certified by the person who reported the testimony.

Rule 75. Venue requirements

(A) Venue. Any case may be venued, commenced and decided in any court in any county, except, that upon the filing of a pleading or a motion to dismiss allowed by Rule 12(B)(3), the court, from allegations of the complaint or after hearing evidence thereon or considering affidavits or documentary evidence filed with the motion or in opposition to it, shall order the case transferred to a county or court selected by the party first properly filing such motion or pleading if the court determines that the county or court where the action was filed does not meet preferred venue requirements or is not authorized to decide the case and that the court or county selected has preferred venue and is authorized to decide the case. Preferred venue lies in:

(1) the county where the greater percentage of individual defendants included in the complaint resides, or, if there is no such greater percentage, the place where any individual defendant so named resides; or

(2) the county where the land or some part thereof is located or the chattels or some part thereof are regularly located or kept, if the complaint includes a claim for injuries thereto or relating to such land or such chattels, including without limitation claims for recovery of possession or for injuries, to establish use or control, to quiet title or determine any interest, to avoid or set aside conveyances, to foreclose liens, to partition and to assert any matters for which in rem relief is or would be proper; or

(3) the county where the accident or collision occurred, if the complaint includes a claim for injuries relating t the operation of a motor vehicle or a vehicle on railroad, street or interurban tracks; or

(4) the county where either the principal office of a defendant organization is located or the office or agency of a defendant organization or individual to which the claim relates or out of which the claim arose is located if one or more such organizations or individuals are included as defendants in the complaint; or

(5) the county where either one or more individual plaintiffs reside, the principal office of a governmental organization is located, or the office of a governmental organization to which the claim relates or out of which the claim arose is located, if one or more governmental organizations are included as defendants in the complaint; or

(6) the county or court fixed by written stipulations signed by all the parties named in the complaint or their attorneys and filed with the court before ruling on the motion to dismiss; or

(7) the county where the individual is held in custody or is restrained, if the complaint seeks relief with respect to such individual's custody or restraint upon his freedom; or

(8) the county where a claim in the plaintiff's complaint may be commenced under any statute recognizing or creating a special or general remedy or proceeding; or

(9) the county where all or some of the property is located or can be found if the case seeks only judgment in rem against the property of a defendant being served by publication; or

(10) the county where either one or more individual plaintiffs reside, the principal office of any plaintiff organization or governmental organization is located, or the office of any such plaintiff organization or governmental organization to which the claim relates or out of which the claim arose is located, if the case is not subject to the requirements of subsections (1) through (9) of this subdivision or if all the defendants are nonresident individuals or nonresident organizations without a principal office in the state.

The pleading or motion permitted by this rule must be filed within the time prescribed for the party making it by Rules 6 and 12 and any other applicable provision of these rules.

(B) Claim or proceeding filed in improper court.

(1) Whenever a claim or proceeding is filed which should properly have been filed in another court of this state, and proper objection is made, the court in which such action is filed shall not then dismiss the action but shall order the action transferred to the court in which it should have been filed.

(2) The person filing the action shall, within twenty (20) days, pay such costs as are chargeable upon a change of venue and the papers and records shall be certified to the court of transfer in like manner as upon change of venue and the action shall be deemed commenced as of the date of filing the action in the original court.

(3) If the party filing the action does not pay the costs of transfer within twenty (20) days of the order transferring venue, the original court shall dismiss the action without prejudice and shall order payment of reasonable attorney fees to the party making proper objection.

(C) Assessment of costs, traveling expenses and attorneys' fees in resisting venue. When the case is ordered transferred under the provisions of this rule or Rule 21(B) the court shall order the parties or persons filing the complaint to pay the filing costs of refiling the case in the proper court and pay mileage expenses reasonably incurred by the parties and their attorneys in resisting the venue; and if it appears that the case was commenced in the wrong county by sham pleading, in bad faith or without cause, the court shall order payment of reasonable attorneys' fees incurred by parties successfully resisting the venue.

(D) Other venue statutes superseded by this rule. Any provision of these rules and any special or general statute relating to venue, the place of trial or the authority of the court to hear the case shall be subject to this rule, and the provisions of any statute fixing more stringent rules thereon shall be ineffective. No statute or rule fixing the place of trial shall be deemed a requirement of jurisdiction.

(E) Appeal. An order transferring or refusing to transfer a case under this rule shall be an interlocutory order appealable pursuant to Appellate Rule 14(A)(8); provided, however, that the appeal of an interlocutory order under this rule shall not stay proceedings in the trial court unless the trial court or the Court of Appeals so orders.

ule 76. Change of venue

(A) In civil actions where the venue may be changed from the county, such change of venue from the county may be had only upon the filing of a verified motion specifically stating the grounds therefor by the party requesting the change. The motion shall be granted only upon a showing that the county where suit is pending is a party or that the party seeking the change will be unlikely to receive a fair trial on account of local prejudice or bias regarding a party or the claim or defense presented by a party. A party shall be entitled to only one change of venue from the county. Denial of a motion for change of venue from the county shall be reviewable only for an abuse of discretion. The Rules of Criminal Procedure shall govern proceedings to enforce a statute defining an infraction.

(B) In civil actions, where a change may be taken from the judge, such change shall be granted upon the filing of an unverified application or motion without specifically stating the ground therefor by a party or his attorney. Provided, however, a party shall be entitled to only one [1] change from the judge. After a final decree is entered in a dissolution of marriage case or paternity case, a party may take only one change of judge in connection with petitions to modify that decree, regardless of the number of times new petitions are filed. The Rules of Criminal Procedure shall govern proceedings to enforce a statute defining an infraction.

(C) In any action except criminal no change of judge or change of venue from the county shall be granted except within the time herein provided. Any such application for change of judge (or change of venue) shall be filed not later than ten [10] days after the issues are first closed on the merits. Except:

(1) in those cases where no pleading or answer may be required to be filed by the defending party to close issues (or no responsive pleading is required under a statute), each party shall have thirty [30] days from the date the case is placed and entered on the chronological case summary of the court as having been filed;

(2) in those cases of claims in probate and receivership proceedings and remonstrances and similar matters, the parties thereto shall have thirty [30] days from the date the case is placed and entered on the chronological case summary of the court as having been filed;

(3) if the trial court or a court on appeal orders a new trial, or if a court on appeal otherwise remands a case such that a further hearing and receipt of evidence are required to reconsider all or some of the issues heard during the earlier trial, the parties thereto shall have ten [10] days from the date the order of the trial court is entered or the order of the court on appeal is certified;

(4) in the event a change is granted from the judge or county within the prescribed period, as stated above, a request for a change of judge or county may be made by a party still entitled thereto within ten [10] days after the special judge has qualified or the moving party has knowledge the cause has reached the receiving county or there has been a failure to perfect the change. Provided, however, this subdivision (4) shall operate only to enlarge the time allowed for such request under such circumstances, and it shall not operate to reduce the period prescribed in subdivisions (C), (C)(1), (C)(2), (C)(3);

(5) where a party has appeared at or received advance notice of a hearing prior to the expiration of the date within which a party may ask for a change of judge or county, and also where at said hearing a trial date is set which setting is promptly entered on the Chronological Case Summary, a party shall be deemed to have waived a request for change of judge or county unless within three days of the oral setting the party files a written objection to the trial setting and a written motion for change of judge or county;

(6) if the moving party first obtains knowledge of the grounds for change of venue from the county or judge after the time above limited, he may file said application, which must be verified personally by the party himself, specifically alleging when the cause was first discovered, how discovered, the facts showing the grounds for a change, and why such cause could not have been discovered before by the exercise of due diligence. Any opposing party shall have the right to file counter-affidavits on such issue within ten [10] days, and the ruling of the court may be reviewed only for abuse of discretion.

(D) Whenever a change of venue from the county is granted, the parties may, within three (3) days from the granting of the motion or affidavit for the change of venue, agree in open court upon the county to which venue shall be changed, and the court shall transfer such action to such county. In the absence of such agreement, the court shall, within two (2) days thereafter, submit to the parties a written list of all counties adjoining the county from which the venue is changed, and the parties within seven (7) days from the date the clerk mails the list to the parties or within such time, not to exceed fourteen (14) days from that date, as the court shall fix, shall each alternately strike off the names of such counties. The party first filing such motion shall strike first, and the action shall be sent to the county remaining not stricken under such procedure. If a party is brought into the action as provided in Trial Rule 14, and that party thereafter files a motion for change of venue which is granted, that party and the plaintiff shall be the parties entitled to strike. A moving party that fails to strike within said time shall not be entitled to a change of venue, and the court shall resume jurisdiction of the cause. If a nonmoving party fails to strike within the time limit, the clerk shall strike for such party.

Rule 77. Court records

(A) Required records. The clerk of the circuit court shall maintain the records for all circuit, superior, and probate courts in the county.

(1) The clerk of the circuit court shall maintain any record required by an act of the general assembly or a duly promulgated rule of any state agency, including the following:

(a) Lis pendens record (IC 32-30-11-1);

(b) Record of transcripts and foreign judgments (IC 33-32-3-2(d));

(c) Judgment Docket (IC 33-32-3-2), wherein all orders requiring entry in the judgment docket shall include the term "judgment" in the title and shall set forth the specific dollar amount of the judgment in the body of the order;

(d) Execution docket (IC 33-32-3-5);

(e) Records specified under the probate code; and

(f) Records specified by the state board of accounts as to the fiscal matters relating to the court and clerk

(2) The clerk of the circuit court shall also maintain the following records as specified under this rule:

(a) Chronological Case Summary (CCS);

(b) Case file;

(c) Record of judgments and orders (RJO or order book); and

(d) Indexes.

(3) Records may be maintained in the following formats:

(a) Paper;

(b) Microfilm, provided the record is authorized to be microfilmed by the provisions of Administrative Rule 7(B) or;

(c) Electronic which means the record is readable through the use of an electronic device regardless of the manner in which it was created.

(B) Chronological Case Summary (CCS). For each case, the clerk of the circuit court shall maintain a sequential record of the judicial events in such proceeding. The record shall include the title of the proceeding; the assigned case number; the names, addresses (including electronic mail address), telephone, and facsimile numbers of all attorneys involved in the proceeding, or the fact that a party appears pro se with address (including electronic mail address), telephone, and facsimile number of the party so appearing; and the assessment of fees and charges (public receivables). The judge of the case shall cause CCS entries to be made of all judicial events. Notation of judicial events in the CCS shall be made promptly, and shall set forth the date of the event and briefly define any documents, orders, rulings, or judgments filed or entered in the case. The date of every notation in the CCS should be the date the notation is made, regardless of the date the judicial event occurred. The CCS shall also note the entry of orders, rulings and judgments in the record of judgments and orders, the notation of judgments in the judgment docket, and file status (pending/decided) under section (G) of this rule. The CCS may be kept in a paper format, or microfilm, or electronically. The CCS is an official record of the trial court and shall be maintained apart from other records of the court and organized by case number, if maintained in a paper or microfilmed format.

(C) Case file. In each case assigned a case number, the clerk of the circuit court shall maintain a file in a single format, unless it is necessary to maintain a case file in a combination of formats to accommodate a filing that cannot be maintained in a single format. The clerk shall make an entry on the CCS if it is necessary to maintain a single case file in a combination of formats. All case files, whether paper or electronic, shall contain a copy of any order, entry, or judgment in the case placed in the RJO, if the clerk is required to maintain a RJO, and the original or electronic copy of all other documents relating to the case: including pleadings, motions, service of process, return of service, verdicts, executions, returns on executions and, if prepared, certified, and approved, the transcript of the testimony. The RJO shall contain the original order, entry, or judgment and the case file shall contain a copy of such original. Unless necessary to detail the filing chronology, the case file need not include transmittal letters, instructions, envelopes or other extrinsic materials unrelated to the issues of the case. The case file, if maintained in a paper format, shall contain an index tab listing the case number and an abbreviated designation of the parties and shall note the information required under section (G) of this rule. In the event the court does not maintain a separate evidence file, documents entered into evidence, including depositions, shall be placed in the case file.

(D) Record of judgments and orders (RJO or order book).

(1) Unless the court has a scanning system approved under Administrative Rule 6 that directly scans or electronically files documents into the court case management system and saves a digital image of a document as part of the electronic case file, the following provisions apply: The clerk of the circuit court shall maintain a daily, verbatim, compilation of all judgments of the court, designated orders of the court, orders and opinions of an appellate tribunal relating to a case heard by the court, local court rules under Trial Rule 81, certification of the election of the regular judge of the court, any order appointing a special judge, judge pro tempore, or temporary judge, the oath and acceptance of any judge serving in the court, any order appointing a special prosecutor, and the oath and acceptance of a special prosecutor. The clerk may maintain a separate RJO as required for the functional management of the court's business. Except where the RJO is maintained electronically, the clerk shall maintain a separate RJO for confidential materials.

(2) If the court has a scanning system approved under Administrative Rule 6 that directly scans or electronically files documents into the court case management system and saves a digital image of a document as part of the electronic case file, the clerk need not maintain a separate RJO.

(E) Indexes. In addition to any index required under the provisions of this rule, state statute, or duly promulgated rule of a state agency, the clerk of the circuit court shall prepare and maintain indexes of all actions and proceedings in the circuit, superior, and, probate courts in the county shall be in an alphabetical format which notes the names of all parties, the date on which a party became part of the proceeding, and the case number of the proceeding. In the event courts are not located in the county courthouse, the clerk shall supervise the appropriate preparation of indexes for these courts and provide for the combination of indexes for all circuit, superior, and probate courts in the county. If the court has a case management system that is searchable by party name, date, and case number, or has the ability to produce an index upon demand, the clerk is not required to prepare and maintain the indexes required by this rule.

(F) Pleadings and papers: Where filed and entered. All pleadings and papers shall be filed in accordance with Trial Rule 5 with the clerk of the circuit court. In the event a court is not located in the same facility as the clerk of the circuit court, all pleadings and papers shall be filed with the clerk serving that court. If an initial pleading or complaint is assigned to a court not within the facility where the initial pleading or complaint was filed, the clerk shall promptly notify the person filing the pleading and transmit the documents to the clerk serving the court where the matter will be considered and all further papers will be filed with the latter court. In the event an initial pleading or complaint is filed with the clerk of the wrong court, the clerk, upon notice to the person filing the initial pleading or complaint, may transfer the case to the proper court before service of summons or appearance of other parties, or any opposing party may move for transfer as provided for under Trial Rule 12(B) or Trial Rule 75.

(G) Case File Status.

(1) The clerk of the circuit court shall maintain the case files, as set forth under section (C) of this rule, in either a pending or decided status. Pending files, arranged by assigned case number, consist of all cases which have not been decided. Decided files consist of the actions which have been concluded and no further proceedings remain to be conducted as evidenced by the final judgment or other order of the court.

(2) When a case has been decided, the file shall be assigned a disposition date pursuant to Administrative Rule 7 of the Indiana Supreme Court and maintained under the original case number in a location apart from pending files. In the event a decided case is redocketed for consideration by the court, the disposition date shall be deleted from the file and the case file returned to the pending cases in sequence with the case number originally assigned. A disposition date shall be reassigned at the time the case returns to a decided status.

(H) Statistics. The clerk of the circuit court shall establish procedures to determine a statistical count of all actions filed, decided, and reinstated as required by the Indiana Office of Judicial Administration (IOJA).

(I) Replacing lost papers. If an original pleading or paper filed with the clerk of the circuit court cannot be located within the recordkeeping system set forth under this rule, the court may authorize a copy of such record to be filed and used as the original.

(J) Method of record keeping. Under the direction of the Supreme Court of Indiana, the clerk of the circuit court may, notwithstanding the foregoing sections, keep records in any suitable media. Records, whether required to be maintained permanently pursuant to Administrative Rule 7 D. (Retention Schedules) (Trial Rule 77 Schedules (10)), or not must, if maintained electronically, be kept so that a hard copy can be generated at any time. All record keeping formats and systems, including case management systems, and the quality and permanency requirements employed for the CCS, the case file, and the RJO (order book) shall be approved by the Office of Judicial Administration for compliance with the provisions of this rule. This Rule applies to court records maintained by clerks, judges, and to judicial branch agencies.

(K) Electronic Posting of Court Records. The clerk of the circuit court, with the consent of the majority of the judges in the courts of record in that circuit, or the clerk of a city, town, or Marion County small claims court, with the consent of the city, town, or Marion County small claims court judge, may make available to the public through remote electronic access such as the internet, those court records approved by the Supreme Court of Indiana for electronic posting. The records to be posted, the specific information that is to be included, its format, pricing structure, if any, method of dissemination, and any subsequent changes thereto must be approved by the Office of Judicial Administration (IOJA) under the direction of the Supreme Court of Indiana. Such availability of court records shall be subject to applicable laws regarding confidentiality.

Rule 78. Jurisdiction pending change from county

Whenever a court has granted an order for a change of venue to another county and the costs thereof have been paid where an obligation exists to pay such costs for such change, either party to the cause may file a certified copy of the order making such change in the court to which such change has been made, and thereupon such court shall have full jurisdiction of said cause, regardless of the fact that the transcript and papers have not yet been filed with such court to which such change is taken. Nothing in this rule shall be construed as divesting the original court of its jurisdiction to hear and determine emergency matters between the time that a motion for change of venue to another county is filed and the time that the court grants an order for the change of venue.

Rule 79. Special judge selection: circuit, superior, and probate courts

(A) Application. When the appointment of a special judge is required under Trial Rule 76, the provisions of this rule constitute the exclusive manner for the selection of special judges in circuit, superior, and probate courts in all civil and juvenile proceedings. Trial Rule 79.1 constitutes the exclusive manner for the selection of special judges in all actions in city, town, and the Marion county small claims courts.

(B) Duty to notify court. It shall be the duty of the parties to advise the court promptly of an application or motion for change of judge.

(C) Disqualification or recusal of judge. A judge shall disqualify and recuse whenever the judge, the judge's spouse, a person within the third degree of relationship to either of them, the spouse of such a person, or a person residing in the judge's household:

(1) is a party to the proceeding, or an officer, director or trustee of a party;

(2) is acting as a lawyer in the proceeding;

(3) is known by the judge to have an interest that could be substantially affected by the proceeding; or

(4) is associated with the pending litigation in such fashion as to require disqualification under the *Code of Judicial Conduct* or otherwise.

Upon disqualification or recusal under this section, a special judge shall be selected in accordance with Sections (D) and (H) of this rule.

(D) Agreement of the parties. Within seven (7) days of the notation in the Chronological Case Summary of the order granting a change of judge or an order of disqualification, the parties may agree to an eligible special judge. The agreement of the parties shall be in writing and shall be filed in the court where the case is pending. Alternatively, the parties may agree in writing to the selection of an eligible special judge in accordance with Section (H). Upon the filing of the agreement, the court shall enter an order appointing such individual as the special judge in the case and provide notice pursuant to Trial Rule 72(D) to the special judge and all parties or appoint a special judge under Section (H).

A judge appointed under this section shall have seven (7) days from the date the appointment as special judge is noted in the Chronological Case Summary to decide whether to accept the case. The filing of an acceptance vests jurisdiction in the special judge. An oath or additional evidence of acceptance of jurisdiction is not required.

This provision shall not apply to criminal proceedings or election contests involving the nomination or election of the judge of the court in which the contest is filed.

(E) Reserved. Deleted, eff. Jan. 1, 2013.

(F) Reserved. Deleted, eff. Jan. 1, 2013.

(G) Reserved. Deleted, eff. Jan. 1, 2013.

(H) Selection under local rule. In the event the parties do not reach an agreement or the agreed upon judge does not accept the case under Section (D), the appointment of an eligible special judge shall be made pursuant to a local rule approved by the Indiana Supreme Court which provides for the following:

(1) appointment of persons eligible under Section J who: a) are within the administrative district as set forth in Administrative Rule 3(A), or b) are from a contiguous county, and have agreed to serve as a special judge in the court where the case is pending;

(2) the effective use of all judicial resources within an administrative district; and

(3) certification to the Supreme Court of Indiana of cases in which no judge is eligible to serve as special judge or the particular circumstance of a case warrants selection of a special judge by the Indiana Supreme Court.

A person appointed to serve as special judge under a local rule must accept jurisdiction in the case unless the appointed special judge is disqualified pursuant to the Code of Judicial Conduct, ineligible for service under this rule, or excused from service by the Indiana Supreme Court. The order of appointment under the local rule shall constitute acceptance. An oath or additional evidence of acceptance of jurisdiction is not required.

(I) Discontinuation of service or Unavailability of special judge.

(1) In the event a special judge assumes jurisdiction and thereafter ceases to act for any reason, except the timely granting of a motion for change of judge, the regular judge of the court where the case is pending shall assume jurisdiction, provided such judge has not previously served in the case and is otherwise eligible to serve. In the event of the timely granting of a motion for change of judge from a special judge or if the regular judge does not assume jurisdiction under this section, a successor special judge shall be appointed in accordance with Sections (D) and (H) of this rule.

(2) In the event that a special judge assumes jurisdiction and is thereafter unavailable for any reason on the date when a hearing or trial is scheduled:

(a) the special judge may, as appropriate, appoint a judge pro tempore, temporary judge, magistrate, or senior judge of the court where the case is pending, provided such judge or magistrate is otherwise eligible to serve and has not previously had jurisdiction of the case removed from them pursuant to the Rules of Trial Procedure, or

(b) the regular judge of the court where the case is pending may assume temporary jurisdiction, provided such judge is otherwise eligible to serve and has not previously had jurisdiction of the case removed pursuant to the Rules of Trial Procedure.

If the regular judge, judge pro tempore, temporary judge, magistrate, or senior judge does not assume jurisdiction under this section, such hearing or trial shall be reset to a date when the special judge is available.

(J) Eligibility. Any regular judge of a Circuit, Superior, or Probate Court, a senior judge, or a person serving as a full-time judicial officer in a court of record, including a person who has been a member of a panel for selection, is eligible for appointment by a trial court as a special judge unless this judicial official:

(1) has previously served as judge or special judge in the case; except that whenever a court has granted an order for a change of venue to another county, the judge granting the change of venue may be appointed as special judge for that cause in the receiving county if the judge granting the change, the receiving judge, and all of the parties to the cause agree to such appointment;

(2) is disqualified by interest or relationship; or

(3) is excused from service as special judge by the Indiana Supreme Court.

A special judge need not be a resident of the county where the case is pending, but accessibility should be considered in making the selection. Senior judges shall be eligible for service as special judge only in courts in which the senior judge is currently appointed by the Indiana Supreme Court to serve as senior judge.

(K) Appointment by Indiana Supreme Court. Upon the certification of a request for appointment of a special judge under Trial Rules 53.1, 53.2, 60.5, I.C. 34-13-5-4, as added by P.L. 1-1998, SEC.8, governing public lawsuits, and this rule, the Supreme Court may appoint any person eligible for service under Section (J) or any member of the Bar of this state as special judge. The order of appointment of a special judge by the Indiana Supreme Court shall be noted in the Chronological Case Summary, entered in the Record of Judgments and Orders, and served on all parties in the proceeding in accordance with Trial Rule 72(D) by the Clerk of the trial court. Such order vests jurisdiction in the special judge, and an oath shall only be required for members of the Bar appointed under this Section.

(L) Continuation of Special Judge Jurisdiction. A special judge shall retain jurisdiction of the case, through judgment and post-judgment, including without limitation, proceedings to enforce the judgment or to modify or revoke orders pertaining to custody, visitation, support, maintenance and property dispositions and post-conviction relief unless:

(1) a specific statute or rule provides to the contrary; or

(2) the special judge is unavailable by reason of death, sickness, absence, or unwillingness to serve.

(M) Transfer of Proceeding. In the event the individual selected to serve as special judge in the case is a regular judge of a court within the county and such court has subject matter jurisdiction of the proceeding, such judge may transfer the case without the assessment of costs to that judge's court for all further proceedings. In the event the individual selected is the regular judge of a court outside of the county where the case is pending and such court has subject matter jurisdiction in like cases, the parties and the judge may agree to a change of venu to such judge's court for all further proceedings. Assessment of statutory change of venue fees shall be shared b the parties as agreed or, failing agreement, as ordered by the court.

(N) Place of Hearing.

(1) Absent the transfer of the case as set forth in Section (M), special judges are encouraged to employ procedures such as the use of facsimile transmissions and telephone conferences that reduce the need for travel.

(2) A special judge may entertain motions and perform all administrative tasks and conferences with counsel in his or her own county.

(3) All hearings involving in-person testimony by witnesses shall be conducted in the court where the case is pending unless:

(a) the parties and the judge agree otherwise on the record, or

(b) the hearing is not before a jury and the special judge determines that exceptional circumstances exist such that the matter can only be heard in a timely fashion in his or her own county.

(4) All decisions, orders, and rulings shall be noted promptly in the Chronological Case Summary and, when appropriate, the Record of Judgments and Orders of the court where the case is pending and shall be served in accordance with Trial Rule 72(D). It is the duty of the special judge to effect the prompt executio of this rule. A court is deemed to have ruled on the date the ruling is noted in the Chronological Case Summary.

(5) It is the duty of the judge of the court where the case is pending to assure the availability of facilities and staff for the special judge.

(O) Emergencies. Nothing in this rule shall divest the original court and judge of jurisdiction to hear and determine emergency matters between the time a motion for change of judge is filed and the appointed special judge accepts jurisdiction.

(P) Compensation. A full-time judge, magistrate, or other employee of the judiciary shall not be paid a special judge fee for service as a special judge. A senior judge shall be paid a special judge fee pursuant to Ind. Administrative Rule 5. All other persons serving as special judge shall be paid a special judge fee of twenty-five dollars ($25.00) per day for each jurisdiction served for the entry of judgments and orders and hearings incidental to such entries. Persons residing outside the county where service is rendered shall be entitled to mileage at a rate equal to other public officials as established by state law, hotel accommodations, and reimbursement for meals and other expenses. Compensation for special judge services shall be paid by the State upon presentation of a claim for such services.

Rule 79.1. Special judge selection: city, town, and Marion county small claims courts

(A) Application. The provisions of this rule constitute the exclusive manner for the selection of special judges in all actions in city, town, and Marion county small claims courts.

(B) Duty to notify court. It shall be the duty of the parties to promptly advise the court of an application or motion for change of judge.

(C) Required affidavit. In any action filed in city, town, or the Marion county small claims courts, notwithstanding the provisions of Trial Rule 76(B), a motion for change of judge shall be verified and signed by the party setting forth facts in support of the statutory basis for the change.

(D) Agreement of the parties. In the event it becomes necessary to appoint a special judge in a city, town, or Marion county small claims court, the parties may agree to the appointment of an eligible individual to so serve. Upon being advised of the agreement of the parties, the court shall appoint such individual as the special judge in the case. This provision shall not apply to criminal proceedings. A special judge selected under this section shall have twenty (20) days to accept jurisdiction, appear, and qualify. The individual who serves as special judge under this section is not entitled to the payment of special judge fees as set forth in Trial Rule 79(J).

(E) Selection by court. Absent an agreement by the parties to appoint a specific individual to serve as special judge, the parties may consent to the appointment of a special judge by the judge presiding in the case. A special judge selected under this section shall have twenty (20) days to accept jurisdiction, appear, and qualify. The individual who serves as special judge under this section is not entitled to the payment of special judge fees as set forth in Trial Rule 79(J).

(F) City and town courts. In the event it becomes necessary to appoint a special judge in a city or town court and the parties fail to agree under Section (D) or (E), the case shall be transferred to the appropriate docket of the county, superior, or circuit court of the county in which the city or town court is located and filed without the assessment of additional fees. The judge who receives the case is not entitled to the payment of special judge fees as set forth in Trial Rule 79(J).

(G) Marion county small claims court. In the event it becomes necessary to appoint a special judge in the Marion county small claims court and the parties fail to agree under Section (D) or (E), the procedure set forth in this section shall apply.

(1) Naming of panel. Within two (2) days of deciding that a special judge must be appointed under this section, the presiding judge shall submit to the parties for striking a panel of three judges, who, pursuant to IC 33-34-5-6 must be other judges of the Marion county small claims court.

(2) Striking from panel. Each party shall be entitled to strike one name from the panel. The moving party shall be entitled to strike first. The parties shall have not less than seven (7) days nor more than fourteen (14) days to strike as the court may allow.

(3) Failure to strike. If the moving party fails to timely strike, the presiding judge shall resume jurisdiction of the case. If a non-moving party fails to timely strike, the clerk of court shall strike in such party's stead.

(4) Transfer of case. Upon completion of the striking process, the case shall be transferred to the court of the judge remaining on the panel without the assessment of additional costs.

(5) Inability to transfer. In the event the case cannot be transferred, for any reason, to the designated special judge, the case shall be transferred to the court having the highest court identifier number, as provided in Administrative Rule 8, of the Marion county small claims court judge who is not disqualified by reason of interest or relationship. No fees will be assessed for such transfer.

(H) Eligibility. Pursuant to IC 33-34-5-6, no person other than a small claims court judge may serve as a special judge in the small claims court. Any regular judge of a circuit, superior, probate, municipal, or county court, a senior judge, or any member of the bar of the state of Indiana is eligible for appointment as a special judge in a city or town court unless this judge or attorney:

(1) has previously served as judge or been a member of a panel for selection as special judge in the case;

(2) is disqualified by interest or relationship; or

(3) is serving as a bailiff, reporter, referee, commissioner, magistrate, or other appointed official of the court where the case is pending, except as expressly authorized by statute.

(I) Continuation of jurisdiction of case. In the event a special judge is appointed or a case is transferred under this rule, the special judge or court shall retain jurisdiction for all future proceedings in the case, including without limitation, proceedings to enforce the judgment and post-conviction relief unless:

(1) a specific statute or rule provides to the contrary; or

(2) the special judge is unavailable by reason of death, sickness, absence, or unwillingness to serve.

Rule 80. Supreme Court Committee on Rules of Practice and Procedure

(A) Creation, members, terms of office, and removal. There is hereby created a committee to be known as the "Supreme Court Committee on Rules of Practice and Procedure" ("Rules Committee"). The Rules Committee shall consist of thirteen members appointed by the Supreme Court. All members of the Committee shall be members of the bar of the state of Indiana.

The term of each member shall be for five years, except that a member appointed to fill the vacancy of an unexpired term shall be appointed only for the remainder of the unexpired term. Any member may be removed by the Supreme Court.

(B) Officers, meetings, quorum, and compensation. Annually, the Rules Committee shall elect from among its members a chairperson who shall preside at all meetings, and a vice-chairperson who shall preside at meetings in the absence of the chairperson. The Court, shall assign such staff as it deems necessary for the Rules Committee to conduct its work, including preparing meeting agendas, taking the minutes of meetings, and maintaining the records of the Rules Committee.

The Rules Committee shall meet monthly at a time and place designated by the chairperson, and the chairperson may call special meetings of the Rules Committee. Seven members shall constitute a quorum at an regular or special meeting. The Rules Committee shall act by a vote of a majority of the members present at any regular or special meeting.

The members of the Rules Committee shall be allowed their necessary expenses and such reasonable compensation as the Supreme Court shall fix from time to time.

(C) Duties of the Rules Committee. The Rules Committee shall conduct a study of any Indiana Rules of Court assigned to them by the Supreme Court and shall submit to the Supreme Court from time to time recommendations in order to promote the just determination of litigation, simplicity in procedure, and the elimination of unjustified expense and delay. The Rules Committee shall also serve as the Evidence Rules Review Committee as set forth in Rule 1101 of the *Indiana Rules of Evidence*.

The Supreme Court shall consider all recommendations and proposed amendments received from the Rules Committee.

(D) Procedure for amending rules. Except in case of an emergency or as otherwise directed by the Supreme Court, the procedure in this section shall be followed in amending the Indiana Rules of Court.

(1) *Submission of proposed rule amendments.* Proposed rule amendments shall be presented to the Supreme Court's Chief Administrative Officer (CAO) in a WORD compatible format, clearly indicating added or deleted language and must be accompanied by the Form available on the Supreme Court's website. The CAO shall provide regular reports to the Chief Justice regarding proposed rule amendments and shall be responsible for referring the proposed amendment to the appropriate committee or other entity for further study.

(2) *Publication of proposed rule amendments.* The Rules Committee shall publish proposed rule amendments on or before January 2, April 1, July 1, and October 1 of each year and at such other times are necessary.

(3) *Comments of the bench, bar, and public.* All comments on proposed amendments from the bench, bar, and public of this state to the Rules Committee shall be delivered in writing to the Rules Committee. Comments received by the Rules Committee shall be confidential unless otherwise ordered by the Supreme Court. The Rules Committee shall accept comments on the proposed amendment for a period of thirty (30) days after publication, and may extend the period for comments. Thereafter, the Rules Committee shall study all comments received and shall submit the proposed final draft of each rule amendment, together with the associated comments, to the Supreme Court for its consideration.

(4) *Publication of amended rules.* The Supreme Court shall be on each proposed rule amendment received from the Rules Committee and shall publish each rule amendment adopted by the Supreme Court. On January 1 of the following year, each rule amendment shall take effect unless the Supreme Court orders otherwise.

Rule 81. Local court rules

(A) Authority. Courts may regulate local court and administrative district practice by adopting and amending in accordance with this Rule local and administrative district rules not inconsistent with--and not duplicative of--these Rules of Trial Procedure or other Rules of the Indiana Supreme Court. Courts are strongly encouraged to adopt a single set of local rules for use in all courts of record in a county and will be required to do so after January 1, 2007. The single set may reflect different practices due to geographic, jurisdictional and other variables. Courts shall not use standing orders (that is, generic orders not entered in the individual case) to regulate local court or administrative district practice. Local and administrative district rules requiring approval of the Indiana Supreme Court or the Indiana Office of Judicial Administration (IOJA) are subject to the provisions of this rule.

(B) Notice and comment.

(1) When a court or administrative district proposes to adopt or amend local or administrative district rules, it shall give notice to the bar and public of the content of the proposal, the time period for the bar and public to comment, the address to which comments should be sent, and the proposed effective date. Notice shall include, but not be limited to, transmitting the proposal to the officers of any local county bar association.

(2) The court shall also transmit the proposal to the county clerk and to the IOJA in digital format. The county clerk shall post the proposal in the county clerk's office(s) and on the county clerk's website, if any, and the IOJA shall post the proposal on the Indiana Judicial Website for public inspection and comment. The court and the IOJA shall receive comments for not less than thirty (30) days.

(C) Schedule. The IOJA shall establish and publish a uniform annual schedule, similar to the schedule for proposed Supreme Court rules under Rule 80(D), for publishing proposed local and administrative district rules, receiving comment, adopting rules, and the effective date of adopted rules.

(D) Exceptions to the schedule. If a court finds that there is good cause to deviate from the schedule established by the IOJA, the court or administrative district may adopt or amend local or administrative district rules at other times. However, a local or administrative district rule shall not take effect unless it has first been posted for thirty (30) days in the county clerk's office(s) and on the county clerk's website, if any, and on the Indiana Judicial Website. The court promptly thereafter shall provide opportunity to comment in the manner provided in subsection (B)(1) above.

(E) Style, format, and numbering. The IOJA shall establish and publish a standard format for drafting and amending local and administrative district rules. The format shall include a uniform numbering system which, to the extent practicable, corresponds to the numbering of these Rules of Trial Procedure and other Rules of the Indiana Supreme Court.

(F) Adopted Rules. The court shall cause adopted rules and amendments to be placed in the Record of Judgments and Orders, shall cause the county clerk to post them in the county clerk's office(s) and on the county clerk's website, if any, for public inspection, and shall transmit a copy of the rules in digital format to the IOJA for posting on the Indiana Judicial Website.

(G) Availability of local and administrative district rules. All local and administrative district rules, as amended and with any appendices thereto, shall be compiled into one document, which shall be posted and available in the clerk's office at all times for public inspection and on the county clerk's website, if any. They shall be available free of charge on the Indiana Judicial Website.

(H) Suspension of local or administrative district rules. In an individual case the court, upon its own motion or the motion of any party, may waive, suspend or modify compliance with any local or administrative district rule if the interests of justice so require. All such waivers, suspensions or modifications shall be entered in the Chronological Case Summary of the case.

(I) Transition. To continue in effect local and administrative district rules promulgated before the effective date of this Rule, the court shall (1) renumber such rules according to the uniform numbering system established by the IOJA under subsection (E) above, (2) cause such rules to be posted and available in the clerk's office as required by subsection (G) above, and (3) transmit a copy of such rules in digital format to the IOJA for posting on the Indiana Judicial Website. By January 1, 2007, local rules must be in compliance with the terms of this Rule.

(J) Periodic review and update. Courts and administrative districts should review periodically and change local and administrative district rules as required by changes in statutes, case law, or these Rules of Trial Procedure or other Rules of the Indiana Supreme Court.

Rule 81.1. Procedures for Cases Involving Family or Household Members

A. Definitions.

(1) An individual is a "family or household member" of another person if the individual:
- (a) is or was a spouse of the other person;
- (b) is or was living as if a spouse or a domestic partner of the other person, this determination to be based upon:
  - (i) the duration of the relationship;
  - (ii) the frequency of contact;
  - (iii) the financial interdependence;
  - (iv) whether the two (2) individuals are or previously were raising children together;
  - (v) whether the two (2) individuals are or previously have engaged in tasks directed toward maintaining a common household; and,
  - (vi) such other factors as the court may consider relevant.
- (c) has a child in common with the other person;
- (d) is related by blood or adoption to the other person;
- (e) has or previously had an established legal relationship:
  - (i) as a guardian of the other person;
  - (ii) as a ward of the other person;
  - (iii) as a custodian of the other person;
  - (iv) as a foster parent of the other person; or,
  - (v) in a capacity with respect to the other person similar to those listed in clauses (i) through (v).(2) "Family Procedures" entails coordination of proceedings and processes, and information sharing among cases in a court or courts involving family or household members.

B. **Type of Cases.** Courts using Family Procedures for a case may exercise jurisdiction over other cases involving the same family or a household member of the family. An individual case to which Family Procedures is being applied may maintain its separate integrity and separate docket number, but may be give a common case number if multiple cases are being heard before one judge. Subject to applicable rules and statutes, the individual cases may all be transferred to one judge or may remain in the separate courts in which they were originally filed.

C. **Notice.** A court intending to use Family Procedures for a case must enter an order notifying all parties of the court's intention and, within thirty (30) days after a case is selected, the court shall provide each party with a list of all cases that have been selected to be heard using Family Procedures.

D. **Designation by Court of Intent to Use Family Procedures and Change of Judge for Cause.** Within fifteen (15) days after notice is sent that a case has been selected to be heard using Family Procedures, a party may object for cause to the designation or selection of a party's case.
Once notice is sent to the parties that a case has been selected to be heard using Family Procedures, no motio for change of venue from the judge may be granted except to the extent permitted by Indiana Trial Rule 76. A motion for change of venue from the judge in any matter being heard in a court using Family Procedures, or any future cases joined in the court after the initial selection of cases, shall be granted only for cause. If a special judge is appointed, all current and future cases in the court proceeding may be assigned to the special judge.

E. **Concurrent Hearings.** A court using Family Procedures may, in the court's discretion, set concurrent hearings on related cases, take evidence on the related cases at these hearings, and rule on the admissibility o evidence for each case separately as needed to adequately preserve the record for appeal.

F. **Judicial Notice.** Indiana Evidence Rule 201 shall govern the taking of judicial notice in courts using Family Procedures.

G. **Court Records Excluded from Public Access.** In a Court using Family Procedures, each party shall hav access to all records in cases joined under this Rule, with the exception of Court Records excluded from Publi Access pursuant to Administrative Rule 9. A party may seek access to such confidential records from another case joined under this Rule in accordance with Administrative Rule 9(G)(7). Records excluded from Public Access shall retain their confidential status and the court using Family Procedures shall direct that confidential records not be included in the public record of the proceedings.

Rule 82. Forms

The forms adopted by the Supreme Court shall be sufficient under the rules and are intended to indicate the simplicity an brevity of statement which the rules contemplate.

Rule 83. Definitions

Subject to additional definitions contained herein, and unless the context otherwise requires, in these rules:

(1) "Court on appeal" means the Indiana supreme court or the court of appeals of Indiana.

(2) "Executive" of a governmental organization includes the governor of the state; the officer or individual occupying any office or unit occupied only by one [1] person; the mayor of any city or town; in the case of a governmental unit or agency headed by more than one [1] person, the presiding officer thereof or the secretary thereof, or if none, any member thereof; in the case of a governmental corporation, the president or presiding officer, secretary, or treasurer thereof. "Executive officer" of an organization includes the president, vice president, secretary, treasurer, cashier, director, chairman of the board of directors or trustees, office manager, plant manager, or subdivision manager, partner, or majority shareholder. For purposes of service of process, notice and other papers, the term includes the personal secretary of any of the foregoing persons or any person employed under or with any of the foregoing persons and who is entrusted with responsible handling of legal papers, and any person employed in the organization if such person promptly delivers the papers served to one of the foregoing.

(3) "Governmental organization" includes the state, or a department, agency, corporation, office or branch thereof; a county, township, municipality or local governmental unit, or a department, agency, corporation, office or branch thereof; or any governmental representative named as such; or any governmental unit.

(4) "Governmental representative" includes an officer, agent, executive or employee of a governmental organization.

(5) "Organization" includes, without limitation, a domestic or foreign corporation, partnership, unincorporated association, business trust, governmental organization or an organization which is a representative.

(6) "Representative" includes, without limitation, a representative of a decedent's estate, guardian, next friend, receiver, assignee for the benefit of creditors, liquidator, trustee or the like.

(7) "Signature" or "signed" includes, without limitation, an electronic reproduction of a handwritten signature.

ule 84. Effective date

hese rules will take effect on January 1, 1970. They govern all proceedings in actions brought after they take effect and lso all further proceedings in actions then pending, except to the extent that in the opinion of the court their application n a particular action pending when the rules take effect would not be feasible or would work injustice, in which event the ormer procedure applies.

ule 85. Vacated

acated Dec. 5, 1995, effective Feb. 1, 1996.

ule 86. Electronic filing and electronic service

(A) Definitions.

(1) *Case Management System ("CMS").* Case Management System is the system of networked software and hardware used by any Indiana court that may receive, organize, store, retrieve, transmit, and display all relevant documents in any case before it.

(2) *Conventional Filing.* Conventional Filing is the physical non-electronic presentation of documents to the clerk or court.

(3) *Electronic Filing ("E-Filing").* E-Filing is a method of filing documents with the clerk of any Indiana court by electronic transmission utilizing the Indiana E-Filing System.
E-Filing does not include transmission by facsimile or by email.

(4) *E-Filing Manager ("EFM").* E-Filing Manager is the centralized entity approved by the Supreme Court that receives and transmits all E-Filing submissions between E-Filing Service Provider(s) and the appropriate Case Management System.

(5) *E-Filing Service Provider ("EFSP").* E-Filing Service Provider is the organization and software selected by a User and approved by the Supreme Court to receive and transmit all E-Filing submissions between the User and the Indiana E-Filing System.

(6) *Electronic Service ("E-Service").* E-Service is a method of serving documents by electronic transmission on any User in a case via the Indiana E-Filing System.

(7) *Indiana E-Filing System ("IEFS").* Indiana E-Filing System is the system of networked hardware, software, and service providers approved by the Supreme Court for the filing and service of documents via the Internet, into the Case Management System(s) used by Indiana courts.

(8) *Notice of Electronic Filing ("NEF").* Notice of Electronic Filing is the notice generated automatically when a document is submitted and transmitted through the Indiana E-Filing System, which sets forth the time of transmission, the name of the court, User, party or attorney transmitting the document, the title of the document, the type of document, and the name of the court, attorney, party, or other person meant to receive the Notice. The time noted in a Notice of Electronic Filing will be the time at the location of the court where the case is pending. A Notice of Electronic Filing will appear immediately on the User's screen upon submission of the document for E-filing.

(9) *Public Access Terminal.* A Public Access Terminal is a publicly accessible computer provided by clerk or court that allows a member of the public to access the Indiana E-Filing System and public court records.

(10) *User Agreement.* A User Agreement is an agreement in a form approved by the Indiana Office of Judicial Administration (IOJA) that establishes obligations and responsibilities of the User within the Indiana E-Filing System.

(11) *User.* User is a Registered User or Filing User.

(a) *Filing User.* Filing Users include court and clerk staff, unrepresented litigants, attorneys, or an agent whom an attorney has expressly designated to make a filing on the attorney's behalf and who has an Indiana E-Filing System user ID, password, and limited authority to file documents electronically.

(b) *Registered User.* A Registered User is a person or entity with a user ID and password assigned by the Indiana E-Filing System or its designee who is authorized to use the Indiana E-Filing System for the electronic filing or service of documents.

(B) User Agreement Required. Every User must execute a User Agreement with one or more Electronic Filing Service Provider(s) before that User may utilize the Indiana E-Filing System.

(C) Commencement of an Action. An action must be commenced:

(1) by using the Indiana E-Filing System unless exempted by these rules;

(2) by paying the filing fee unless the fee is waived by an order of the court; and

(3) by filing the complaint or equivalent pleading and the required summons(es) in the form set out in Trial Rule 4(C).

(D) Electronic Filing of Documents.

(1) Unless otherwise permitted by these rules, all documents submitted for filing in courts identified in the *E Filing Implementation Schedule* posted at http://courts.in.gov/efile (as updated from time to time) must be filed electronically with the clerk using the Indiana E-Filing System. The e-filing of documents shall be controlled by the case number in the Indiana Electronic Filing System designated by the User.

(2) Attorneys or unrepresented litigants who wish to be exempted from the requirement that they file electronically may file a petition for electronic filing exemption. The petition must be filed in each pendin case to which these rules are applicable. The petition will be reviewed by the judicial officer assigned to that case and granted only upon a showing of good cause.

(E) Proof of Filing. Users should print or otherwise save each Notice of Electronic Filing as proof of E-Filing. Confirmation of E-Filing may also be made by referring to the Chronological Case Summary of the court in which the case is pending through the Case Management System of that court.

(F) Conventionally Filed Documents. Conventionally filed documents must be converted into an electronic record by the clerk or court. The filer must also conventionally serve these documents in accordance with these Rules and applicable Local Rule(s) and file a certificate of service. If the original documents cannot be convertec into a legible electronic document, then annotation must be made in the Chronological Case Summary and the documents returned to the filer.

A person filing a will for probate shall file an accurate and complete copy of the will and an affidavit, signed under the penalties of perjury, containing substantially the following information:

(1) Affiant possesses the Decedent's original Last Will and Testament or the Will has been deposited with the clerk of the court;

(2) Affiant is filing a true and accurate copy of the Last Will and Testament;

(3) Unless the Last Will and Testament has been deposited with the clerk of the court, Affiant will retain the original Last Will and Testament until the Decedent's estate is closed and the Personal Representative is released from liability, or the time to file a will contest has expired, whichever is later; and,

(4) Affiant will file the original Last Will and Testament upon order of the court or as otherwise directed by statute.

(G) Service of Pleading and Other Papers:

(1) Except as otherwise provided in this Rule, all process shall be served in accordance with Trial Rules 4 and 4.1 through 4.17.

(2) *Issuance of Summons and Service of Initial Complaint or Equivalent Pleading.*

(a) At the time the initial complaint or equivalent pleading is filed, the filer shall also file completed summons(es) designating the manner of service. The Clerk shall date, sign and seal the summons(es) and transmit the summons(es) to the filer for service.

(b) The filer shall serve the initial complaint or equivalent pleading and the summons upon all parties in the manner provided in Trial Rules 4.1 through 4.14.

(c) In the event of service by registered or certified mail, or other public means by which a written acknowledgement of receipt may be requested and obtained, or first class mail (as provided in Trial Rule 4.1(B)) the filer shall promptly transmit to the Clerk a dated and signed Certificate of Issuance of Summons specifying the method of service with respect to each party, the date of mailing, address of each party, and tracking or identifying number for each summons.

(d) All returns regarding service shall be directed and made to the Clerk.

(i) If service was issued under Trial Rule 4.1(A)(1), the filer shall note the case number on each return receipt or equivalent form. If service by mailing or other public means is returned without acceptance, the Clerk shall reissue the summons(es) and complaint or other equivalent pleading for services as requested by the person seeking service.

(ii) If service was made by the filer personally delivering the summons and complaint or equivalent pleading to a party under Trial Rule 4.1(A)(2), the served party shall execute an acknowledgment of service that the filer shall promptly transmit to the Clerk. If the served party fails to execute an acknowledgement of service, the filer shall promptly execute and transmit a dated and signed Affidavit of Service to the Clerk.

(iii) If service was made by the filer leaving a copy of the summons and complaint or equivalent pleading at the dwelling house or usual place of abode of the party under Trial Rule 4.1(A)(3), the filer shall complete service as required by Trial Rule 4.1(B) and promptly transmit a dated and signed Affidavit of Service to the Clerk.

(iv) If service was made by Sheriff or other authorized police officer, constable or appointed process server, the person making service shall promptly make his or her return upon or attach it to a copy of the summons and deliver it to the Clerk, all as provided in Trial Rule 4.15(A).

(e) For service by publication the filer, in addition to filing the complaint or equivalent pleading and summons(es) designating service by publication, shall also transmit an affidavit for service by publication to the Clerk as provided in Trial Rule 4.13. The Clerk shall transmit to the filer dated, signed and sealed summons(es) by publication. The filer shall deliver the summons(es) to the publication authorized by Trial Rule 4.13(C), with instructions that after the completion of the period of publication the return shall be sent to the Clerk.

(f) When fees and other court costs are waived, and the clerk has received the required notification that the filer is entitled to this waiver, the clerk shall serve the complaint and summons(es). Additionally, for service of separate or additional summons (alias summons) by the clerk, the filer shall provide documentation establishing that the filer is entitled to waiver of the fee for service.

(3) *Service of Subsequent Pleadings*

(a) *Service on Registered Users.* Registered Users must serve all documents in a case upon every other party who is a Registered User through E-Service using the Indiana E-Filing System. E-Service has the same legal effect as service of an original paper document. E-Service of a document through the Indiana E-Filing System is deemed complete upon transmission, as confirmed by the Notice of Electronic Filing associated with the document. Exempt parties must serve all documents in a case as provided by Trial Rules 4 or 5.

(b) *Service on Others.* Trial Rules 4 and 5 shall govern service of documents on attorneys of record and on unrepresented parties who are not Registered Users.

(H) Format Requirements.

(1) Documents filed electronically must be formatted in conformity with this Rule and the requirements of the Indiana E-Filing System.

(2) All documents must be submitted in the manner required by the E-Filing Service Provider. The Indiana E-Filing System may be accessed via any Internet connection available to the Registered User and at Public Access Terminals located in the offices of the county clerk.

(I) Signature.

(1) All documents electronically filed that require a signature must include a person's signature using one of the following methods:

(a) a graphic image of a handwritten signature, including an actual signature on a scanned document; or

(b) the indicator "/s/" followed by the person's name.

(2) A document that is signed and E-filed must be subject to the terms and provisions of Trial Rule 11(A). A Registered User may include the Signature of other attorneys in documents E-filed with the court but in doing so represents to the court that any such Signature is authorized.

(J) Time and Effect. Subject to payment of all applicable fees pursuant to Section (C), a document is considered E-filed with the court on the date and time reflected in the Notice of Electronic Filing associated with the document. E-Filing must be completed before midnight to be considered filed that day, and compliance with filing deadlines is determined in accordance with the time zone in the location of the court where the case is filed.

E-Filing under these rules shall be available 24 hours a day, except for times of required maintenance.

(K) Official Court Record. The electronic version of a document filed with or generated by the court under this rule is an official court record.

(L) Clerk Processing of E-filed Documents.

(1) The clerk may reject an e-filing only when:

(a) the applicable filing fee has not been paid; or

(b) the filer selected an incorrect case management system; or

(c) the filer requests rejection.

(2) If an e-filed document cannot be electronically processed, the clerk shall return it to the User for correction through the IEFS. The User may cure the defect within seventy-two (72) hours from the time of return as set out in the notice of return.

(3) In all other cases where an e-filed document does not conform to the IEFS or other applicable rules, the clerk must process the e-filed document and may direct the non-conforming document to the intended E-Filing court. A court that receives a non-conforming document shall:

(a) strike the non-conforming document; or

(b) issue an appropriate order. If the court's order allows a party to cure a defective E-Filing, the party has seventy-two (72) hours, to cure the defect.

(4) In the event a user submits a cured document within seventy-two (72) hours, excluding days the court is closed, the document is timely filed.

(M) Certain Court Records Excluded From Public Access.

(1) Procedures for Excluding Court Records From Public Access. Any User filing a Court Record that is to be excluded from Public Access must do so in accordance with the following procedures:

(a) Notice to maintain exclusion from Public Access.

(i) In cases where the Court Record is excluded from Public Access pursuant to Administrative Rule 9(G)(1)(b,c), 9(G)(2), 9(G)(3), or 9(G)(4), the party or person submitting the confidential record must provide the separate written notice required by Administrative Rule 9(G)(5)(a) identifying the specific 9(G)(2) or 9(G)(3) ground(s) upon which exclusion is based. (See Administrative Rule 9(G) Forms 9-G1 and 9-G2.)

(ii) In cases where all Court Records are excluded from Public Access in accordance with Administrative Rule 9(G)(1)(a), no notice of exclusion from Public Access is required.

(b) Public Access and Non-Public Access Versions. Where only a portion of the Court Record has been excluded from Public Access pursuant to Administrative Rule 9(G)(2) or 9(G)(3), the following requirements apply:

(i) Public Access Version.

a. If a document contains confidential Court Records to be excluded from Public Access, that confidential Court Record shall be omitted or redacted from this version.

b. The omission or redaction shall be indicated at the place it occurs in the Public Access version. If multiple pages are omitted, a separate place keeper insert must be inserted for each omitted page to keep PDF page numbering consistent throughout.

c. If the entire document is to be excluded from Public Access, the Administrative Rule 9(G)(5)(a) Notice filed with the document will serve as the Public Access Version.

(ii) Non-Public Access Version.

a. If the omitted or redacted Court Record is not necessary to the disposition of the case, the excluded Court Record need not be filed or tendered in any form and only the Public Access version is required. The Administrative Rule 9(G)(5)(a) Notice shall indicate this fact. (See Administrative Rule 9(G) Form 9-G3.)

b. If the omitted or redacted Court Record is necessary to the disposition of the case, the excluded Court Record must be separately filed or tendered as follows.

1. The first page of the Non-Public Access Version shall be conspicuously marked "Not for Public Access" or "Confidential," with the caption and number of the case clearly designated.

2. The separately filed Non-Public Access version shall consist of a complete, consecutively-paginated replication including both the Public Access material and the Non-Public Access material.

3. Use of green paper is abolished for E-Filing. Pages in the Non-Public Access version containing Court Records that are excluded from Public Access shall instead be identified with a header, label, or stamp that states, "CONFIDENTIAL PER A.R. 9(G)" or "EXCLUDED FROM PUBLIC ACCESS PER A.R. 9(G)."

(iii) The requirements in Rule 86(M)(1)(b) do not apply to cases in which all Court Records are excluded from Public Access pursuant to Administrative Rule 9(G)(1).

(2) E-filing document security codes settings.

(a) Where only a portion of the Court Record has been excluded from Public Access pursuant to Administrative Rule 9(G)(2) or 9(G)(3), the e-filing document security codes setting for the Public Access Version shall be "Public Document."

(b) Where only a portion of the Court Record has been excluded from Public Access pursuant to Administrative Rule 9(G)(2) or 9(G)(3), the e-filing document security codes setting for the Non-Public Access Version shall be "Confidential document under Admin Rule 9."

(c) In cases in which all Court Records are excluded from Public Access pursuant to Administrative Rule 9(G)(1), the e-filing document security codes setting shall be "Confidential document under Admin Rule 9."

(N) Inability to E-File.

(1) Indiana E-Filing System Failures.

(a) The rights of the parties shall not be affected by an Indiana E-Filing System failure.

(b) When E-Filing is prevented by an Indiana E-Filing System failure, a User or party may revert to conventional filing.

(c) With the exception of deadlines that by law cannot be extended, when E-Filing is prevented by an Indiana E-Filing System failure, the time allowed for the filing of any document otherwise due at the time of the Indiana E-Filing System failure must be extended by one day for each day on which such failure occurs, unless otherwise ordered by the court.

(d) Upon motion and a showing of an Indiana E-Filing System failure the court must enter an order permitting the document to be considered timely filed and may modify responsive deadlines accordingly.

(2) Other Failures Not Caused by the User Who Was Adversely Affected. When E-Filing is prevented by any other circumstance not caused by the User who was adversely affected, the User may bring such circumstances to the attention of the court and request relief as provided in Trial Rule 6(B), or the User may revert to conventional filing.

(O) Appearance Form in E-Filed Cases. In all e-filed cases the parties shall file an appearance as provided in Trial Rule 3.1, with the following modifications:

1. The appearance form shall omit the statement contained in Trial Rule 3.1(A)(4) regarding acceptance of service by FAX or by e-mail.

2. The appearance form shall contain:

a) Certification that the contact information listed on the Indiana Supreme Court Roll of Attorneys for each attorney is current and accurate as of the date the appearance is filed;

b) Acknowledgment that orders, opinions, and notices, and all documents served under Trial Rule 86(G) will be sent to the attorney at the email address(es) on the Roll of Attorneys regardless of other contact information supplied by the attorney; and

(c) Acknowledgment that each attorney listed on the appearance is solely responsible for keeping his/her Roll of Attorneys contact information accurate per Ind. Admis. Disc. R. 2(A).

(See Form 86-1.)

Form		
Appendix A Schedule and Format for Adoption of Local Court Rules, Pursuant to Trial Rule 81	n/a	Adobe PDF
Appendix A-1 Request for Approval of Local Rules	n/a	Adobe PDF
Appendix A-2 Affidavit of Debt	Microsoft Word	Adobe PDF
Appendix B Appearance by Attorney in Civil Case	Microsoft Word	Adobe PDF
Appendix C Guardianship Registry Information Sheet	Microsoft Word	Adobe PDF
Form 86-1 E-filing Appearance by Attorney in Civil Case	Microsoft Word	Adobe PDF

Made in the USA
Monee, IL
26 February 2021